ESSEX RAILWAY HERITAGE

Supplement

Peter Kay

CORRIGENDA AND ADDENDA TO THE FIRST VOLUME

p.3 (re Stour Valley line locations). Bartlow station building was also in Essex but is now in Cambridgeshire.

p.5 (re building of the Brentwood - Colchester line). No work was started east of Brentwood until spring 1841 (contracts for all sections Margaretting to Springfield had been let in December 1838 – January 1839, but had then been 'suspended'; the remaining contracts were not let until February – April 1841). Most (not all) bridges had been completed by autumn 1842.

On 28.10.1842 the ECR Board resolved to end Braithwaite's services on 1.2.1843, and he 'resigned' in January 1843; but in fact he continued to do some work after this, and was clearly on good terms with all at the time of the opening to Colchester in late March.

p.5 (list of viaducts). Chelmsford Station Viaduct has *45* arches west of Duke Street.

p.10 (re Sancton Wood and Thompson). Delete second sentence in the Sancton Wood section and replace by

'It was unfortunate for Sancton Wood that the ECR Board decided that the 1843 Colchester line stations beyond Brentwood should have only 'temporary' wooden buildings, the ECR's financial problems putting an end to any ideas of a sequence of grand stations such as was no doubt envisaged in 1836. Only Shoreditch, Stratford, and Ilford received good permanent buildings before the money problems struck (although Brentwood and Ingatestone were added in the next period of easy money in 1845/6). Wood must really have been very frustrated by his ECR commission'. [See also p.135].

With regard to the Cambridge line, it is quite likely that Wood and Thompson were working in harmony on the stations between Newport and Brandon; Wood may have sought assistance owing to commitments elsewhere. It is probably futile to try to identify individual Cambridge line stations as purely 'Wood' or purely 'Thompson'. The termination of Wood's services in October 1845 was part of a general clear-out of existing senior figures at the start of the Hudson regime, and need not be seen as involving any perceived failings on his part.

p.10 Harlow Mill station building *did* originally have a shaped gable in the right-hand pavilion.

p.11 (re Audley End and Great Chesterford) – change 'verandah' to 'awning'.

p.12 Wickham Bishops station house has in fact been greatly altered and extended since the 1960s.

p.14 Chappel Viaduct – Bruff's November 1845 Deposited Plans show a viaduct only 792ft long.

p.17 Dovercourt. The centre section of the building was originally topped by a large open belfry (as Chelmsford and Bures) - see photo at p.61 of *Images of England, Harwich and Dovercourt.* The pediment that now tops the 'stump' was originally on top of the belfry.

p.18 Thorington station building, although in the same style, is not a direct 'copy' of any Norwich & Spalding Railway station (see p.137).

p.21 Loughton station was all white brick (see p.96).

The reference to the house section in all '1865' station buildings being 'the same' is to be modified by the comments at p.94.

p.23 Marks Tey down platform building originally had an awning on all four sides.

p.24 (top caption). '1865' level crossing houses the same as that at Easton Lodge were built at several other locations between Shelford and Sudbury in addition to Glemsford. They had porches similar to that at Easton Lodge, which makes it likely that these porches were an original feature.

p.26 (bottom). The Great Eastern Hotel is now 'Quayside Court'.

p.30 (top caption). For the Ingatestone canopy see photo p.81.

p.33 (middle caption). Woodham Ferrers was also to the Rochford / Southminster design, see p.139.

p.34 (top caption). The detached Station Master's house at Cold Norton also survives.

p.38 The outside crane at Chappel was brought here by the EARM. It had previously been at Harwich & Dovercourt Sailing Club from the 1950s to 1985. They had received it from Stowmarket station but it is not certain that it had been in use there. The original timber jib was replaced by the present tubular steel jib (which came from the BR ship *Arnhem*) in the Sailing Club period.

p.41 The present triple glass canopy at Witham should have been noted as a 1976 replacement; for the original see p.141.

p.44 For more on the Ingatestone, Newport, Wivenhoe and Great Bentley canopies see p.110.

p.45 There are no known examples of 'Mk I' standard valancing in Essex dating from its original period c1878-1884, however there are/were aberrantly-late examples at Debden (1892 – p.91), Cressing (1892 – p.105), and Roydon (1895?).

p.49 It appears that the Debden footbridge never had any roofing pre-LT.

p.51 Add to list of surviving New Essex Lines type cottages in middle caption 'Two pairs at Cold Norton'.

p.52/3 Change '1912-15 type' to '1911-15 type', and add to list of cottages of this type 'Chelmsford, Widford Road two pairs, 1912 and 1914'. Change total from 45 to 'at least 49'.

p.53 Mount Bures crossing house is in fact inhabited despite its appearance.

p.54 The school at Parkeston was in the event built in 1888 by the Ramsey School Board and *not* by the GER (hence its decidedly non-Ashbee appearance).

p.58 Drawings of East Ham station in *The Railway Engineer* May 1906 include a specific statement that James Robertson was responsible for its design, thereby confirming that it was he who designed later LT&SR station buildings.

p.64/5 New station buildings Earls Colne 1904/5 not 1903/4.

p.66 Marks Tey goods shed is 1865.

p.70 (Shenfield photo). The buildings (but not the canopy) on platforms 3/4 are largely 1886, see p.78.

p.71 The bricks used for all the 1940 buildings at Loughton are *rebated at the top* (not chamfered).

Right Chelmsford viaduct

The first volume

ESSEX RAILWAY HERITAGE
THE COUNTY'S RAILWAY BUILDINGS AND THEIR HISTORY

WITH AN INTRODUCTION TO GREAT EASTERN RAILWAY ARCHITECTURE

was published in 2006 and is still available, price £9.95, from bookshops or post free from publisher (address on inside front cover, cheques to P. KAY).

A further volume

EAST LONDON RAILWAY HERITAGE

to be published at a future date, will cover GER and LT&SR buildings in 'Essex in London' plus Tower Hamlets. If you are interested in this publication, please advise the publisher (preferably by email) and you will be advised when publication is imminent.

Contents

Gazetteer of Surviving Railway Buildings and Structures in Essex

* indicates closed lines

[.......] means 'exclusive'

Introduction To Supplement Volume

This Supplement volume lists the surviving railway buildings and structures in Essex (boundary as defined in the Introduction to the main volume), in line order as set out opposite. It can virtually be regarded as a 'census' of what existed in 2006, however it should be noted that some of the more out of the way locations have not been visited since 2001-4.

All station and other buildings are included except very small huts, late C20 huts, and small platform shelters of post-1940s date.

A more selective approach has been taken with bridges, not just because of their number - there are over 600 railway bridges in the county - but also because so many of them have been reconstructed since the 1950s in connection with electrification, and are therefore no longer of any historic interest. Older bridges are included only if they remain basically in original 1840s-1880s condition, or retain some significant interesting features from that period. A few of the larger or more significant later bridges are also included. All station footbridges are included. Bridges on the GER system were and are consecutively numbered in a system dating from 1911, and these numbers appear on a plate on each bridge. On the ex-LT&SR lines a different system is used with a separate sequence for each line. London Underground have their own numbering system and these numbers are given here for the Ongar line in addition to the GER number.

Where buildings or bridges are not publicly accessible or visible, this is noted (not infallibly). Unfortunately many overbridges are now virtually invisible at road level owing to the mass growth of trees and bushes in recent years, and in consequence can only be seen in fleeting glimpses from a passing train.

Some recently-demolished structures are specifically noted as such in the Gazetteer, to give positive confirmation of this.

There is inevitably some repetition here of facts already given in the main volume; this has been kept to a minimum, with cross-referencing here where longer accounts are already available there.

As explained in the Introduction to the first volume, it was originally intended that these books would be restricted to buildings still in existence. However, it became evident on further thought that, at least so far as station buildings are concerned, it would not be difficult to extend the coverage to buildings now demolished. This has been done in an Appendix at the end of this volume. It needs to be emphasised that this extension of coverage does not (with odd exceptions) apply to *other* types of building and structure. [A full account of GER signal box designs is already available in *The Signal Box: A Pictorial History and Guide to Designs* (OPC, 1986). Other types of GER building have yet to be researched in full].

'Further Reading' references are given in all cases where a station has been dealt with elsewhere in articles or books. Where the facts as given here differ from those in previous publications, this is a deliberate correction based on further research.

The pages in this volume are numbered in the same sequence as the main volume, to simplify cross-referencing. In view of the large amount of cross-referencing, plus the fact that the main volume covers everything in historical order and the Supplement covers everything in location order, it has not been thought necessary to provide an Index.

In addition to those already named in the first Introduction, I would like to thank Graham Austin, Nigel Bowdidge, Rodger Green, Bruce Keeling, Mike Stanbury, Andy Wallis, and all who contributed to the 'Corrigenda'. Andy Rush has done a lot more work in supplying photographs and extracting all the data from the GER bridge records. The book has again been put together by Jim Connor who also supplied much other assistance and encouragement.

Photographs where not credited to the contrary were taken by the author, and where not otherwise dated (or obviously older) were taken in 2001-2007.

Peter Kay
Wivenhoe, June 2007.

Kelvedon viaduct (Bridge 187) in more spacious days (*cf* p.6) showing the covered pedestrian way to the low level station, added in 1904 and removed after closure of the Tollesbury line. This viaduct proved difficult to construct owing to poor soil conditions. Braithwaite's February 1842 report noted that an arch had collapsed, sheet piling was required, and the river had flooded the site.

GAZETTEER

1. COLCHESTER MAIN LINE, BRENTWOOD TO MANNINGTREE

BRENTWOOD

[For 1845 main building demolished 1932 see p.135].

Main building 1933, two-storey, red brick. See photo p.70; the road frontage has been rather mauled latterly although the Venetian window survives.

[Separate 1933 up side B.O. building was destroyed by bomb].

1845 ECR buildings on down side platform 4, in largely original state (photos p.8 and here). Short extension of this block at west end, 1933, in 1933 style. Canopy on this platform 1884, with 'GER' brackets, mostly supported on the building wall but three bays at centre are full-width on columns of Buckhurst Hill (see p.43) type. Valancing 1934.

1933 platform buildings and canopies on middle island platform 2/3.

Up side platform 1 retains only two bays of 1933 canopy [remainder of canopy, and all platform buildings, demolished].

Footbridge, plate steel, 1933.

Further Reading - GE Journal 92, British Railways Illustrated Annual No.5.

BRIDGE 123 (Seven Arch Bridge), overbridge, Seven Arches Road / Hartswood Road, GR 601930. 1842/3. For photo and details see p.8. Almost invisible at road level.

Platform side view of the Brentwood 1845 buildings and the 1884 canopy. At left a glimpse of the 1933 extension. Since this photograph was taken in 2002 the 1934 valancing has had several inches cut off and now ends just below the line of holes.

A recent view of the 1845 down side buildings at Brentwood (the eastern end, seen at left in p.8 photo). The former 'Booking Office' doorway (which may not have been original anyway) has been bricked up. The ridge tiles and finials have done well to survive.

BRIDGE 124 (Three Arch Bridge), overbridge, Ingrave Road, GR 604932. 1842, yellow brick, standard three-arch overbridge, three segmental arches, centre arch 26ft span side arches 21ft 6in span, 149ft long. Widened on both sides with girders.

BRIDGE 124A (Thrift Wood footbridge), GR 611939. 1933, three-span lengthy lattice footbridge.

BRIDGE 125, overbridge, Woodway, GR 612943. 1842, yellow brick, standard three-arch overbridge, three segmental arches of 26ft span, 136ft long.

SHENFIELD

[For 1886 street level building demolished 1932, see p.139].

c1972 BR office block on street frontage incorporating Booking Hall.

1933 platform buildings and canopy on down side platform 5 (photo p.70).

The buildings on island platform 3/4 are 1886, heavily altered in 1933. The main block originally had a hipped roof, which was cut down to below eaves level in 1933 and a new flat roof installed to fit under the new canopy (which was wholly new 1933). The windows and doors are mainly original 1886; the flat-arched 1886 windows look very similar to those installed in wholly new 1933 buildings, but they have small-paned upper sashes and plate glass lower sashes, whereas new 1933 windows have small-paned upper and lower sashes. The 1886 and 1933 brickwork is also difficult to distinguish. There were originally no doors on the NW side of the building, which faced the embankment pre-1933, but two of the original doors were moved to this side in 1933 to give direct access from the new Up Local platform. The smaller block at the London end of the platform (now Train Announcer's office) was originally the 1886 goods lock-up (with hipped roof, as those at the New Essex Lines stations); it was reduced in width and in length in 1933 and given a flat roof.

1979-81 platform buildings and canopy on up island platform 1/2.

1981 temporary signal box (red brick relay room type structure with sloping roof).

Further Reading - British Railways Illustrated Annual No.5 (this also has a photograph of the 1933 street frontage building removed c1970).

BRIDGE 127, underbridges, Hutton Road / Rayleigh Road, GR 614951. 1932/3, typical of the work done on the Romford - Shenfield quadrupling. Three girder spans side-by-side. Continuous retaining wall between the bridges, in engineering brick.

GER COTTAGES in Rayleigh Road / Alexander Lane. Five semi-detached pairs at junction of Rayleigh Road and Alexander Lane (numbered as part of Rayleigh Road), Nos 2/4 (photo p.51) and 10/12 are c1886, Nos 6/8 14/16 and 18/20 are 1901/2 to same design.

Later cottages further down Alexander Lane - No.10 1915 (of the 1911-15 standard type, greatly altered and extended), Nos 11/12 1905 (photo p.86).

BRIDGES 128 and 743S and 743N, underbridges, Alexander Lane, GR 617955. As Bridge 127.

WHITEGATES EMERGENCY CONTROL CENTRE building, 1939.

BRIDGE 129, underbridge, River Wid alias Chain River, GR 626966. 1842, referred to by Pasley as a single semicircular arch 'viaduct', it is actually a 21ft6in span tunnel through the embankment. Approachable on east side but hardly visible owing to concrete extension on this side.

Continued on p. 80

1842 UNDERBRIDGES SHENFIELD TO CHELMSFORD

top left
Bridge 130 is largely in original condition (albeit defaced by the usual modern road signage). The brickwork has some recent patching, especially in the wing wall at left.

second left
Bridge 133 is one of the least altered of the remaining 1842 Colchester line bridges, with very little patching (however the parapet wall is all a reconstruction). Unusually the wing walls are of *convex* plan.

third left
The netherworld of Bridge 134. The arch is original but the rest of the brickwork is heavily refaced.

bottom left
The up side portals of the 'Bridge 141' tunnels. The footpath tunnel has a curved staircase at this end, up to the lane from which it is accessed. This tunnel has a headroom of only 6ft and as it is of course also unlit, it provides a now-rare bit of fun away from the Health & Safety nutters!

top right
Bridge 144 spans the estate drive to Killigrews house. It is not clear why it had to be built on the skew as the drive has a sharp bend here anyway. The construction must have been somewhat defective as the whole of the arching had to be reconstructed later in engineering brick, with six rings (the inner two of which seem to be additional). This view shows well how the coursing is arranged in a skew bridge. The wing walling here is quite lengthy because of the skew.

bottom right
Bridge 146, the single-arch River Wid 'viaduct'. This bridge too had to be significantly strengthened later. The whole of the arching was rebuilt in blue bricks, with no less than eight rings. On the up side, seen here, the original yellow brick facing remains above the arch, but on the down side the whole of the brickwork above the arch is also replacement blue bricks.

top left

The replacement 1840 Almshouses at Ingatestone were not of course a 'railway' building, even if they were effectively paid for by the ECR; but they merit illustration here because of their architectural influence on the 1846 station buildings. They are in a similar red brick, but with white brick dressings against the station's stone dressings. The Almshouses' diaperwork is more skilfully done, and they must win on overall charm, but the station's lozenge-pattern windows perhaps have the edge over the Almshouses' simple diamond pattern.

top right

Detail of one of the 1846 windows at Ingatestone station.

below

Ingatestone station roofscape, showing all the 1846 building's gables. At bottom the flat roofed Gents; the low gabled section is the Ladies; the main longitudinally-gabled section covers the Booking Hall/Office; and the transverse gabled section is the Station Master's house.

BRIDGE 130, underbridge, Lower Road, GR 627967. 1842, brownish brick, 101ft long 20ft span semicircular-arch 'tunnel'.

BRIDGE 132, overbridge, Church Road, GR 633975. 1842, brownish brick, three 34ft span three-centred arches. At 32ft height this is the second highest overbridge on the line, but it is not well seen from road level.

BRIDGE 133, underbridge, Burnthouse Lane, GR 640982. 1842, brownish brick, 20ft 6in span slightly horseshoe arch.

BRIDGE 134, underbridge, 'Tanhouse Brook', GR 642984. 1842. Another stream 'tunnel' like Bridge 129. It originally served an occupation road also, which explains why a bridge for a minor brook was built so, instead of as a small culvert. Yellow brick, 25ft span semicircular arch. Approachable from up side by unofficial footpath from Burnthouse Lane. Photo p.79.

INGATESTONE

Signal box, GER Type 7, 1904, new uPVC windows and boarding, locking room bricked up.

Gate cottage, assumed 1846, in same style as station building (photo p.53).

Main station buildings 1846, see p.9. Several windows have replacement plain glazing, and some alterations to chimneys, otherwise largely in original state. Restoration 1989. Small extension to house section at country end, c1890, distinguished by lack of diaperwork. Booking Office / Hall interior arrangement/ screen believed 1872, also old doors and fireplaces.

Late C19 single-storey flat-roofed extensions at SW end of buildings, now used as cycle shed.

c1850s yellow-brick gabled hut adjacent to footbridge (photo p.48), original purpose not known, latterly lamp room.

Footbridge 1886, raised 1950s, see p.48.

Up platform buildings and canopy 1885, see pp.29/30 and p.110. Canopy still at full width.

Yellow brick platform wall behind up platform to east of footbridge.

Further Reading - GE Journal 87.

BRIDGE 137, overbridge, Fairfield, GR 652994. 1884, wrought iron girders on red brick abutments.

BRIDGE 138, overbridge, Stock Lane, GR 654996. 1842, yellow brick, standard three-arch overbridge, three 28ft span segmental arches, 22ft high.

STOCK LANE. Almshouses, 1557, purchased by ECR and used as Booking Office for the first Ingatestone 'station' 1843/4 (see p.5).

GER cottages, two semi-detached pairs, 1903 (see p.52).

BRIDGE 141, underbridge, 'Clark's Bridge', GR 672011. 1842, reddish-yellow brick. This actually comprises two adjacent 132ft long tunnels through the high embankment, each with a 7ft span horseshoe arch. The northern tunnel is for a footpath and the southern tunnel for a stream. Photo p.79.

BRIDGE 143, underbridge, Maldon Road, GR 678017. 1842, yellow brick, 21ft span semicircular (slightly horseshoe) arch.

BRIDGE 144, underbridge, Killigrews, GR 687031. 1842, yellow brick, 21ft span skew arch, whole of arch reconstructed (early C20?) in engineering brick. Photo p.79.

HYLANDS (GR 688036), GER COTTAGES. Pair of semi-detached cottages, unique (?) design with gable to road, standard GER canopies above front doors. Built for signalmen, date not known but post-1896. [This is the pair furthest from the line; the pair nearest the line do not look GER].

BRIDGE 146, underbridge, River Wid (and occupation road), GR 692042. 1842, yellow brick, single 40ft span arch, long wing walls. Accessible from public footpath on east side of line. Photo p.79.

BRIDGE 147, overbridge, Widford Road, GR 697052. 1842, yellow brick, originally three 26ft span segmental arches with stone voussoirs, centre arch replaced by concrete span c1955. Almost invisible from road level.

GER COTTAGES in Widford Road. Two pairs, one pair at west end of bridge, the other pair at east end of bridge. One pair 1912, the other pair 1914 (not known which is which). Photo p.86.

BRIDGE 148, overbridge, Writtle Road, GR 699059. 1842, yellow brick, standard single-arch overbridge, 33ft 9in span three-centred arch. Widened with C20 concrete span on SW side. Original bridge can only be seen from up trains (almost invisible at road level).

Platform view of the 1885 Ingatestone up side building and canopy. As with the later Southend line stations, the Booking Hall doorway on the platform side is segmental-arched, but the windows on this side are all flat-arched.

above
Detail of the 'string course' brickwork on the 1885 Ingatestone up side building.

below
This 1920s view of Ingatestone up side has now come to light, confirming the existence of a canopy over the road side doorway as postulated at p.30. It is set higher than the Wivenhoe canopy, but is to the same design apart from the usual differences in the carving of the struts.

Graham Austin collection

The northeast end of the Chelmsford (Can) viaduct, showing the simple end pilasters and the substantial wing walls. Braithwaite's August 1841 report noted that 'the foundations were laid'; by August 1842 'nine of the arches are turned (six are centred),nine remain to be completed'.

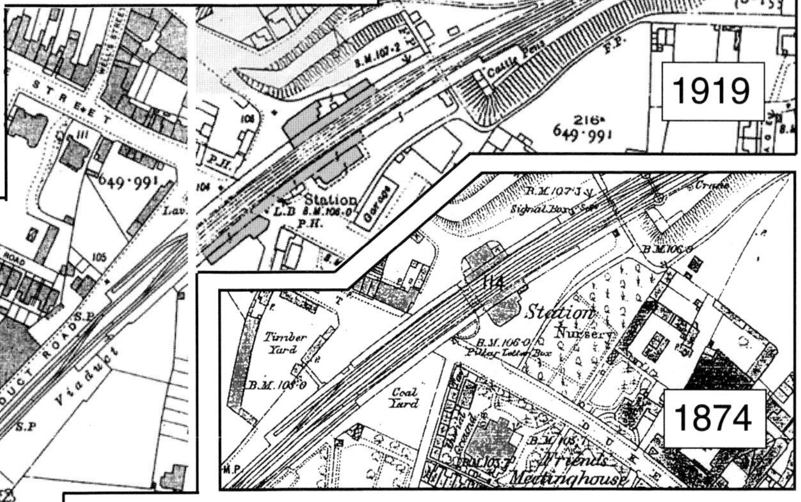

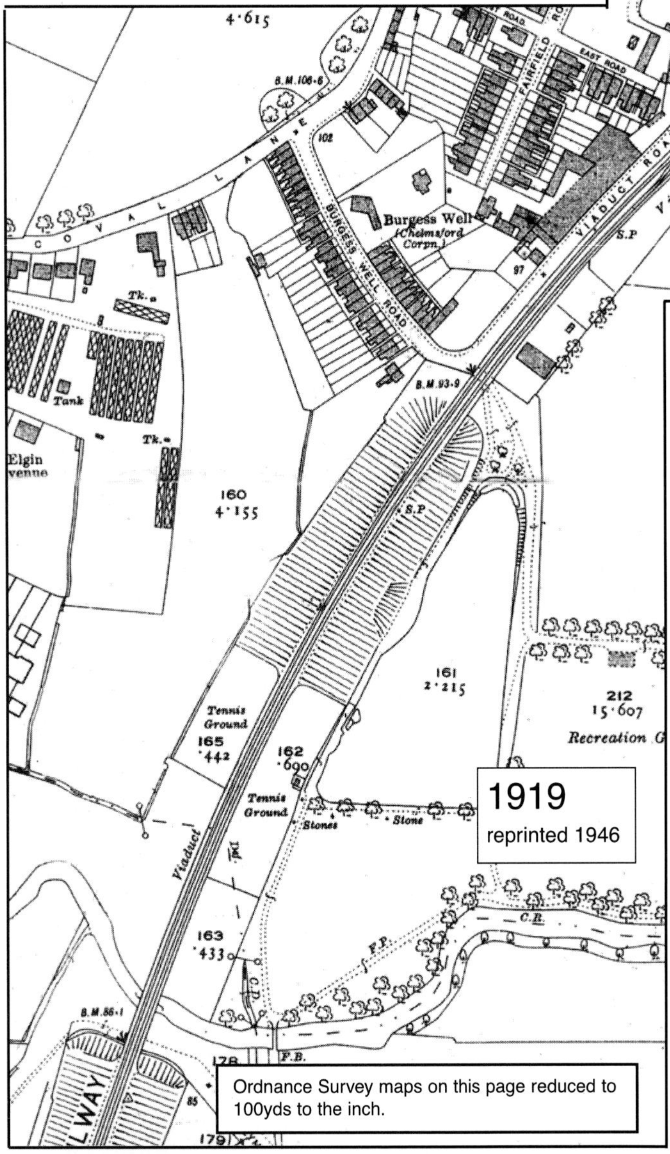

Ordnance Survey maps on this page reduced to 100yds to the inch.

Arches 51 (left) to 32 in the double track section of the Chelmsford Station viaduct. The parapet wall on this side ends at the pillar between arches 47 and 46. Its removal must have been due to the installing here (by 1851) of a short up siding (supported on an *ad hoc* widening of the viaduct that has now been removed).

BRIDGE 149, CHELMSFORD (RIVER CAN) VIADUCT. 1842. See pp.5-6.

BRIDGE 150, CHELMSFORD STATION VIADUCT. [Duke Street bridge is numbered separately - see below]. 1842, altered 1856. Reddish-yellow brick, semicircular arches, 4 rings. Height reduces from 30ft at Parkway to 19ft at the NE end. The total length including Duke Street bridge is 1428 ft making it the longest stretch of continuous viaduct in Essex. There are some sections of solid walling in addition to the 62 numbered arches.

The first 700ft from the London end, arches 62 to 30, is 29ft 6in wide, i.e. normal double track width. The piers all have a single relieving arch. Only arches 62 to 58 (photo p.6) and arch 50 (photo below) are now left open; the others have all been boarded or blocked in and let as industrial units.

The remainder of the viaduct, twelve arches west of Duke Street and seventeen arches east of Duke Street, appears to have consisted originally of two separate single-track viaducts with a gap between them. No engineering drawings are actually known showing it so, however all the visible piers (plus the Duke Street abutments) have an obvious infill section in the middle, assumed to date from 1856 when the station was reconstructed. There are three relieving arches in each pier, one in each of the original viaducts and the middle one in the infill section. The overall width is 62ft throughout this section and this was always the distance between the outer faces (*cf* Braithwaite's November 1841 Engineer's report 'the Chelmsford viaduct is widened for the station to 62ft'). In the present station entrance area two of the arches are used as public and passenger subways and two others are accessible forming the route to the passenger lifts.

BRIDGE 151, underbridge, Duke Street. 1842. See p.6 and p.84.

CHELMSFORD

An outline account of the station's development is necessary to appreciate what remains. [NB - this station has been little researched hitherto, and the account here cannot be regarded as the final word on the subject]. The original 1843 island platform arrangement, with access by stairs up from Duke Street between the two bridges, was very radical for its date, and was developed by Braithwaite from first principles to avoid the dangers then normally inherent in passengers having to cross the tracks to reach the opposite platform (this was before the general introduction of footbridges). By 1851 there were three timber-built Office / Waiting Rooms blocks on the island platform, not all of them necessarily original. One guesses that these blocks and the platform itself were supported on girders between the two viaducts (?). Nothing remained of these structures after 1856, except that one of them was re- erected as a house in Broomfield Road (see GE Journal 33).

In 1856 the station was converted to a side platform arrangement, with very narrow platforms and four tracks between them (as shown on the 1874 OS map here), the platforms being served by 'loops'. This was later altered to two running lines and a single central siding. New station buildings were provided on both the up and down sides in 1856; the main entrance block on the up side (photo below) lasted until 1987, and the down side block is still in situ. The basic plan of the station today remains as in 1856.

In 1899 the platforms were widened and new canopies (still in situ) provided. The 1856 buildings on both sides were enlarged, and additional office / platform buildings provided behind the up platform west of Duke Street. The 1919 OS map here shows the '1899' situation.

In 1987/8 a wholly new up side entrance building was constructed on the site of the 1856/1899 building.

What exists today, therefore, is
1987/8 entrance building at road level
1856 down side buildings, enlarged 1899
1899 three-storey office block and up platform buildings west of Duke Street
1899 'standard` platform canopies (with new 1980s roofing). Supported on columns throughout, with small solid longitudinal brackets. *plus*
Platform wall behind east end of down platform, 1881
Signal box, on tall brick base, 1899, disused since 1996 (see p.68)
Water tank behind east end of down platform, 1881 (see p.67).

Further Reading - GE Journals 33 and 88.

Continued on p. 85

Arch 3, one of the low arches at the NE end of the Chelmsford Station viaduct.

Looking SW through the relieving arches of the 1842 down line portion of the viaduct at the same point.

Chelmsford up side in the 1920s, showing the buildings demolished in 1987. The left hand section with the belfry is the 1856 building; the narrower right hand section, built in a similar style, is the 1899 extension. The belfry was later removed, otherwise there was little change into the 1980s. The arch that formed the public subway to Railway Street (left) prior to 1987 has now become Smith's shop.

Plans for the rebuilding of Chelmsford station were submitted by Bruff to the ECR Permanent Way & Works Committee in November 1855.

Graham Austin collection

right

Despite the efforts of the Luftwaffe, this 1943 view is the best that has been found of the Chelmsford 1856 down side building prior to the alterations of 1987/8. The central portion incorporated the Station Master's house, hence the front door and garden.

The extensions at either end of the building, which are in a lighter brick, must represent the 1899 work (although maps are a little unhelpful).

Graham Austin collection

top left

The down side buildings in 2004. The main changes made in 1987/8 were (1) the bricking up of the Station Master's house door and a large first floor window and two small second floor windows above it (2) insertion of two windows vice one in the second floor, r/h end of main section (now Waiting Room) (3) archway at right (vice ground floor windows) for the new public subway.

second left

The up side of Duke Street bridge. The rear wall of the platform above is 1899, in connection with the new platform canopies. At left is the 1899 three-storey office block which is in a darker yellow brick. (Although referred to here for convenience as '1899', the new works at Chelmsford seem to have been spread over a two year period. The 'rearrangement of Chelmsford station' was approved by the GER Board in December 1897, the main contract was let to A.J. Bateman in July 1898, and the Board of Trade inspection was in July 1899, but it was noted then that the new buildings were not yet completed). The office block has a chamfered corner to enable Park Street to debouch without having to demolish the *Railway Tavern*. The conspicuous four-course 'quoins' of this block are in the same dark yellow brick as the rest.

third left

These canopy brackets were reused in the 1987/8 work. They must date from 1899 as they are identical to those on the 1899 Bishops Stortford up side Booking Office building (p.47). However the 1856 up side building had always had a road side canopy.

below

The new up platform buildings of 1899 west of Duke Street, for which the viaduct had to be widened for a four-arch length. They were clearly built as part of the same job as the office block.

below (two photos)

Underview of Duke Street bridge showing the stone voussoirs, quoins, plinth and imposts of the original 1842 up line arch, and (far left) the 1856 central section with its wholly brick construction. (NB: There is a gap between these two photographs.)

left

The amusing (6ft headroom) footpath 'tunnel' Bridge 152 beneath the road approach embankment from Railway Street to the original 1840s goods shed. The tunnel is in yellow brick but the retaining wall for the high level goods yard (right) is in red brick. The parapet wall above the tunnel has been recently refaced in red brick.

BRIDGE 152, footpath subway under old goods yard, GR 706072. 1840s, horseshoe arch, 3 rings. Photo p.84.

BRIDGE 154, RIVER CHELMER VIADUCT, GR 714075. See pp.5-6.

GER COTTAGES off Arbour Lane (GR 717076). Terrace of ten cottages, 1912. Built by E. Willmott & Sons for £2,035. Plans for these cottages exist at ERO, ref. D/B7/Pb495. Now Nos 104-122 Arbour Lane. Photos p.86.

BRIDGE 156, overbridge, Stump Lane, GR 719077. 1842, yellow brick, standard single-arch overbridge, 33ft span three-centred arch.

BRIDGE 161, BOREHAM MILL VIADUCT, GR 747099. 1842, red brick, four three-centred arches of 30ft span and 10ft rise, 26ft high. Photo p.87.

BRIDGE 164, overbridge, Chantry Lane, GR 767109. 1842, red brick, standard single-arch overbridge, 33ft 9in span three-centred arch, skew.

BRIDGE 167, RIVER TER VIADUCT, GR 781117. Referred to by Pasley as 'Hatfield Mill viaduct'. 1842, three three-centred arches of 40ft span and approx. 15ft rise, 46ft high (the second highest of the Colchester line viaducts). Heavily patched. Photo p.87.

HATFIELD PEVEREL

Main building/Station Master's house 1878 (see p.25). 1980s extension at west end for new toilets. Small road side entrance canopy, and brick extension beneath it, C20. Small canopy above Booking Hall doors on platform side, c1930?

Goods lock-up (to east of house), hipped roof, late C19.

Footbridge, concrete, c1960.

[Original down platform structures demolished].

One pair semi-detached cottages, 1880 (see p.50).

BRIDGE 173, overbridge, Job's Wood (occupation), GR 800131. C20 girder central span (previously timber span), four 1842 yellow brick 14ft 8in span semicircular arch side arches (two either side). Not accessible.

BRIDGE 174, underbridge, Blunts Hall Road, GR 812143. 1842, red brick, 14ft 10in span semicircular arch. See p.7.

BRIDGE 176, underbridge, footpath. GR 816147. 1842, unique pale yellow brick, 23ft 1in span semicircular-arch 'tunnel'. See p.7.

BRIDGE 177, RIVER BRAIN VIADUCT (also over Almond Road), GR 818150. See pp. 5-6.

WITHAM

All the station buildings at Witham belong to the 1907 rebuilding (except for the lift towers which are mid-C20 brick replacements). The red brick Booking Office building is carried on girders over the down loop line, supported on a pier faced in engineering brick. Photo p.41 shows the present appearance at road level with 1976 replacement canopy, photo p.141 shows the original flat canopy. The island platform buildings are in red brick with a two-course waistband in engineering bricks. 'Standard' platform canopies. The down island canopy is supported entirely on 'large circle' brackets on the walls; it has cut-back valancing on the platform 3 side but original valancing on the platform 4 side. East of the platform buildings the roofing is altered, with a ceiling. The up island canopy is supported on columns (with small solid longitudinal brackets) on the platform 2 side (photo p.47 top left), and on 'large circle' wall brackets on the platform 1 side (photo p.47 top right); it has full original valancing throughout. Footbridge, lattice span, has Crittall's maker's plates ('Crittall Coy Constructional Engineers Braintree').

Signal box, BR(ER) Type 18, 1960, abolished as SB 1996, now used as offices.

BRIDGE 182, overbridge, Crakers Lane alias Cranes Lane, GR 849180. Yellow brick 33ft 7in span three-centred arch of only two rings. The use of yellow brick this far east, and the non- standard construction, suggest that this is not an original 1842 bridge. However there was *a* bridge built here in 1842.

BRIDGE 184, overbridge, Rolley Lane, GR 859189. 1842, red brick, standard single-arch overbridge, 33ft 8in span three-centred arch. Additional early C20 semicircular arch on north side, faced in engineering brick.

Continued on p.88

COLCHESTER LINE COTTAGES

top left

Nos 11-12 Alexander Lane, Shenfield, largely unaltered except for the inevitable replacement windows. The design is the same as the Manningtree cottages at p.52, except the ground floor windows are set two courses higher here and in consequence the 'keystones' are smaller.

second left

The western pair of cottages at Widford Road bridge. They are in yellow brick, except for red brick ground floor window arches, and are to the standard design of 1911-15 (p.52). The eastern pair of cottages differ in having flat-arched ground floor windows.

third left and below

The Arbour Lane cottages. Like the Widford cottages they are of the 1911-15 type.

MORE 1842 BRIDGES, CHELMSFORD TO COLCHESTER (see also pp. 6-8)

above Boreham Mill viaduct, up side. (There are four arches - the central pier is shown twice in this composite view). With its original parapet wall remaining, this (along with the Chelmer viaduct) is the best-preserved of the 1842 Colchester line viaducts. The arching is in red brick (original?) but otherwise the same brownish-yellow brick as used west of Chelmsford features.

below Detail of the imposts and 7-ring arches, River Ter viaduct. Most of the facing bricks seen here are relatively recent pinkish-red patching; the original work (of which some can be seen in the spandrels here) is in a yellowy-red brick. This viaduct can be reached by a footpath from the B1137 that passes underneath the A12, however the trees below the viaduct are too dense to permit any good view of it.

second right The unique Bridge 199. As well as the single-ring arch, this bridge also has a two-course string course different from that on the standard 1842 bridges.

third right Bridge 198 from the south. The design is very similar to Bridge 130.

fourth right Bridge 204, up side view. The pilasters here are a little wider than at Bridge 174, and the wing walls continue higher than the string course above the arch.

two page spread bottom Bridge 194 seen from the public recreation ground on the south side of the A120. There have been several changes to this bridge over the years. The four sloping buttresses on this side are in a different brick to the walling and are therefore probably not original. The whole of the parapet walls seem to have been rebuilt in 1959 (they are in a much lighter brick). The three semicircular arches faced in engineering brick in the angled wall carrying the bridge girders are probably late GER work, but the upper portion of this wall in light red bricks must be 1959 in connection with the present concrete spans.

right
Ordnance Survey 25in map of Marks Tey, 1919 survey. Buildings extant in 2006 are shaded black. Bridge 194 appears at the west end of the extract.

below (two photos)
The Gas Plant at Marks Tey. On the east side the windows are of '1865' pattern, and the quoins are also '1865'.

below right
The Marks Tey up platform canopy.

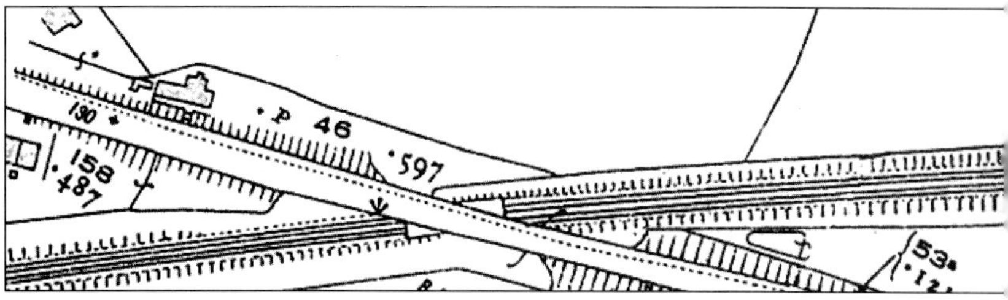

KELVEDON

[For 1871 station building demolished 1990, see p.138].

Station building 1990. Footbridge, concrete, c1960. Station Master's house 1890/1 (contract to A.Coe November 1890 at £459), badly altered.

BRIDGE 187, RIVER BLACKWATER VIADUCT (also over Station Road), GR 863193. See pp.5-6.

BRIDGE 191, overbridge, New Lane ('Hanover Bridge'), GR 876205. 1842, red brick, standard single-arch overbridge, 33ft7in span three-centred arch. Photo p.7.

BRIDGE 194, overbridge, Coggeshall Road (A120), GR 912236. This bridge was regarded as a work of note in 1842, as the turnpike road was kept on its original alignment, necessitating a considerable skew. The original lengthy red brick walls survive on the south side. There were originally two cast iron girder spans with central columns between the tracks (the only use of iron girders for an original overbridge on the Brentwood – Colchester section). The present concrete spans date from 1959 when the road was widened. Photo pp. 86/7.

MARKS TEY

Small single-storey Booking Office building, c1970 (when the now-demolished 1864 main up side building – photo p. 96 – was taken out of use).

Up platform canopy and rear wall (which represents the middle one-third of the full length of canopy that existed from 1901 to the 1960s) is of early date with columns of a type not known elsewhere, but had 'standard' valancing fitted in 1901. (This canopy cannot be 1864 but was erected prior to the 1875 OS).

Down platform has unique '1865' style building, 1864 (photo p.23). Small white brick building on down platform to the west of this, date and purpose not known.

Gas Plant behind down platform, assumed 1864, derelict.
Footbridge, concrete, c1960.

Goods Shed, 1865, timber (see photo in GE Journal 77 for original appearance). Now rendered and much altered externally.
GER curved-roof brick hut in car park near Goods Shed.

BRIDGE 198, underbridge, Turkey Cock Lane, GR 933247. 1842, red brick, 20ft2in span 79ft long semicircular-arch 'tunnel'.

BRIDGE 199, overbridge, occupation road/footpath ('Fenner's Bridge'), GR 939249. Although of similar outline to the standard type of 1842 single-arch overbridge, this bridge is extraordinary in having only a single-ring arch, and therefore may not be 1842. Red brick, 34ft span three-centred arch. Photo p.87.

BRIDGE 200, overbridge, 'Wagstaff's Bridge', GR 944252. 1842, standard three-arch overbridge, three 28ft span segmental arches. Lower parts original red brick, upper parts reconstructed and faced in engineering brick (photo p.8).

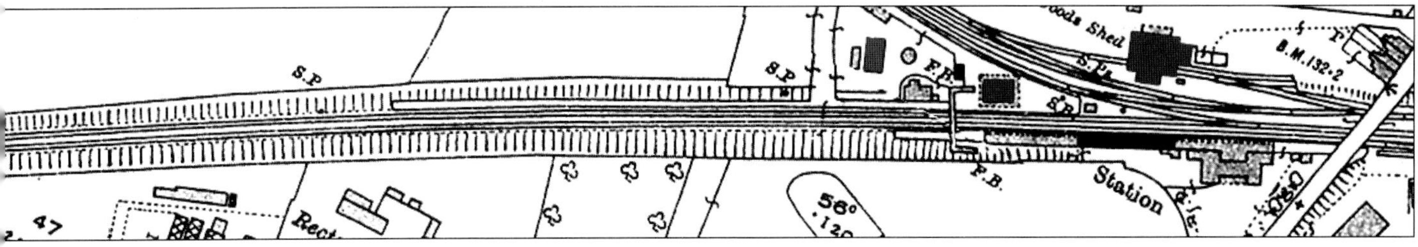

BRIDGE 202, overbridge, Iron Latch Lane, GR 954256. 1842, red brick, standard three-arch overbridge, three 32ft span segmental arches. Invisible at road level.

CHITTS HILL LEVEL CROSSING. Gatekeeper's hut, brick, curved roof, c1900.

BRIDGE 203, SEVEN ARCH VIADUCT (River Colne), GR 963261. See pp. 6-7.

BRIDGE 204, underbridge, 'Phillips' Bridge', GR 968263. 1842, red brick, 15ft span semicircular arch, pilasters and wing walls similar to Bridge 174. Photo p.87.

BRIDGE 205, overbridge, Baker's Lane, GR 973265. 1842, red brick, standard three-arch overbridge, three 28ft span segmental arches. Invisible at road level.

COLCHESTER

Main up side building 1895/6, see pp. 39-40. Single storey extensions at both ends in red brick, c1960.
Steel canopy on platforms 3/6 1939.
Steel canopy on platforms 4/5 1961.

Down island platform and red brick platform buildings and canopy 1961.
Down side entrance hall and offices behind 1961 (later became Booking Office).

Lower portion only of 1962 power signal box.
Signal box, red brick, 1983.
Diesel shed, c1961.
Range of single storey white brick workshops (to north of down side entrance), built in several phases 1870s-1890s.
Single storey red brick workshops building to east of last, c1900s.

Colchester Electric Feeder Station (GR 997263, up side). 1958. Of interest only in being the UK's first 25kv installation.

BRIDGE 209, underbridge, occupation/footpath, GR 008263. 1845, built by ECR, red brick 'tunnel'.

ARDLEIGH

[No remains of station buildings].
Station Master's house, GER, 1865, red brick. Contract to Perry & Jackson 13.10.1864 at £575. Rewindowed. Photo p.90.

BRIDGE 223, underbridge, Mill Hill, GR 077318. 1846 (EUR), red brick, 20ft3in span segmental arch, skew. Photo p.90.

BRIDGE 224, underbridge, Lawford Hall occupation road, GR 088322. 1846 (EUR), red brick, 12ft span semicircular arch.

MANNINGTREE

Main building on up side 1899/1900 (see p.41). 'Standard' canopy (reduced in length at east end), supported on columns throughout, small solid longitudinal brackets. Original glass remains in 'Refreshment Room' and 'General Waiting Room' windows (photo p.4).
At west end of up platform a separate small 1899/1900 hipped-roof building, used latterly as cycle store.

The later of the workshops ranges at Colchester down side, in red brick. The wall in the foreground, although rebuilt in engineering brick, represents the face of the 1843 cattle pens platform, and is the only surviving relic of the 1843 station.

The footpath tunnel Bridge 209 is the only significant bridge structure on the two and a half miles of line beyond Colchester (as far as GR 031274) built by the ECR in 1845 and sold to the EUR. The tunnel is 129ft long; the arch is of 10ft span and has six rings.

Down side building 1899/1900. Original glass remains in 'Ladies Waiting Room' and 'General Waiting Room' windows (photo p.41). [Down platform canopy wholly removed c1979].
[Goods Shed demolished].
Stables, c1900, see p.66.
Water tank/tower 1894, see p.67.
Two pairs of cottages, 1905, see p.52.

BRIDGE 228, underbridge, River Stour Viaduct, Cattawade. There are two viaducts at Cattawade, this (the western) is half in Essex and half in Suffolk, the other Bridge 229 over Cattawade Creek is wholly in Suffolk. Both date from 1903/4 and are to the same design; they replaced the original much-repaired timber viaducts. The contract was let to The Horseley Co in March 1903 at £13,771. Photo p.90.

top left
The 1865 Ardleigh Station Master's house, now 'Station House'.

bottom left
Bridge 223.

top right
Bridge 224.

bottom right
The end of Essex – Bridge 228 from the Essex bank.

2. ONGAR LINE, BUCKHURST HILL TO ONGAR

BUCKHURST HILL

Station house (south of Queens Road), 1856, ECR Loughton branch standard type, red brick, rewindowed. Now LUL offices. Portion (the northernmost one-third) of 1856 down platform remains adjacent.

Queens Road pedestrian subway, completed 1942.

Main station building 1891/2, see p.35.

At south end of up platform, 1881/2 timber-fronted Waiting Rooms plus canopy with 'GER' brackets and sawtooth valancing (see p.43). Contract to W.Bangs 18.10.1881 at £795. Remainder of up platform rear brick wall and canopy, and whole of down platform buildings/rear wall and canopy, 1891/2. Buildings behind down platform have segmental-arched windows. 'Standard' canopies, supported on columns, with small solid longitudinal brackets (an early example).

Footbridge 1891/2, lattice, unique design.

BRIDGE 689/o60, overbridge, Palmerston Road/Roding Lane, GR 418940. 1856, red brick, three-centred arch. Upper parts rebuilt and parapet walls raised late C20.

LOUGHTON

[For 1865 building demolished c1940, see photo p.96].

Main building at road level and platform buildings and concrete canopies 1940 (see p.71).

Signal Box built 1940/1 opened 1948, LT standard type, now disused. [The 59-lever Westinghouse power frame has gone to the London Transport Museum].

Electric Substation 1940 (at east end of station; west of Roding Road on up side), now disused as such and converted to staff accommodation.

BRIDGE 697/o73, underbridge, Alderton Hall Lane, GR 433957. 1865, red brick, 11ft9in span segmental arch. Widened c1891 on up side in yellow brick. Photo p.92.

DEBDEN

House section only remains of '1865' 'small' type building of 1865 [remainder demolished 1973]. All white brick. Rewindowed.

Main building on down side LT 1973/4, single storey with flat roof.

Down platform canopy 1973/4.

1865 white brick rear wall behind west end of down platform.

Up platform building 1892, heavily altered 1973. Up platform canopy 1973.

Footbridge 1891, lattice, see p.49. Roofing 1974.

Second footbridge at east end of platforms c1956 as access route for Bank of England Printing Works, lattice.

Signal Box opened 1949, LT standard type, red brick, now disused.

Terrace of four cottages 1896 (Nos 30/32/34/36 Chigwell Lane). Photo p.50.

BRIDGE 700/o77, VIADUCT over Cole Brook (no official name known). GR 448968. 1865, five 20ft span semicircular arches.

Widened (on up side) 1890/1. Original section red brick. 1890/1 section faced in engineering brick. Photo p.92.

Coal Duty Obelisk, on up side (at foot of embankment), GR 452977. (Not actually a railway structure).

BRIDGE 701, overbridge, 'Cattle Bridge', GR 454986. 1865, three cast iron spans 20ft6in/25ft/20ft6in, brick piers and parapet wall. Photo p.92.

THEYDON BOIS

Main building (down side) '1865' 'medium' type, 1865, red brick with white brick dressings, house section roughcast on west and south sides by 1960s. Booking Office section extended 1940s into under-canopy area on road side and window altered (photo p.22). Scullery (in garden) 1865.

Down platform canopy 1884, supported by 'GER' brackets on walls. Canopy extended at both ends by LT and original section given plain valancing to match.

Up platform building, '1865' single-storey 'other platform' 'medium' type, 1865, red brick with white brick dressings. Small 1940s extension south end. (Theydon Bois had two platforms from the start but the up platform was not brought into use for passenger purposes until 1884).

Up platform canopy 1884, supported by 'GER' brackets on walls. Canopy extended at both ends by LT and original section given plain valancing to match.

Red brick walls behind both ends of both platforms, 1865 (some parts recently rebuilt).

Footbridge, lattice, 1885 (see p.48).

BRIDGE 703/o87, underbridge, Bridge Hill, GR 460009. 1865, red brick, 25ft9in span segmental arch. Widened c1891 on down side, red brick. Upper parts of 1865 portion strengthened 1990s with jettied-out parapet wall. Photo p.92.

EPPING

Main building (down side) '1865' 'large' type, 1865, all red brick. House section extended 1891. Road side canopy is LT replacement (1949?). Platform side covered area heavily altered late C20. Scullery (in garden), 1865. Photos p.95.

Small flat-roofed Station Master's office building on down platform to north of main building, c1890.

Small yellow brick gabled building, original function not known, on down platform to south of main building, 1880s.

New waiting shelter on down platform, 2007.

Up platform building '1865' single-storey 'other platform' 'large' type, 1865, all red brick, much altered. 1940s extension north end.

Footbridge, lattice, 1892 (see p.49). 'Westwood Baillie & Co. Ltd Engineers 1892' maker's plates. Roofing removed.

Red brick walls behind both platforms, 1865.

Signal Box, LT, 1949, now disused. Taken over by preservation group. [1949 Westinghouse power frame was removed prior to this, but the frame from Hainault is to be moved here].

Electric Substation, 1949? (south of station on up side).

BRIDGE 705/o94, overbridge, Bower Hill, GR 463017. 1865, red brick, three 25ft span segmental arches, skew.

BRIDGE 706, overbridge, Stonards Hill, GR 468021. 1865, red brick, three segmental arches. The road falls to the SE and as a result the arches spring at different heights. This bridge is in good original condition but is difficult to appreciate owing to tree growth.

BRIDGE 707, overbridge, footpath/occupation, GR 473026. 1865, three cast iron spans 20ft/25ft/20ft, reddish-yellow brick piers and parapet wall (same design as Bridge 701).

Buckhurst Hill footbridge and canopies. The footbridge has 'A.Handyside & Co 1891 Derby' maker's plates. The Mk II 'standard' valancing at this station is without holes.

The intact 1865 building at Debden in March 1973. The station rebuilding commenced in April. *J.E. Connor*

Another March 1973 view of Debden, showing the 1892 up platform building and canopy, then still in original condition. This station had only one platform originally (the 1865 'small' type buildings were only erected at single-platform stations). The up platform was added in 1891/2 when the line was doubled from Loughton to Epping. This canopy was notable for having Mk I 'standard' valancing, an aberration at this late date (but *cf* Cressing p.105).

NORTH WEALD

Main building '1865' 'small' type, 1865, all red brick (photo p.95). Gents (1865?) at west end. Scullery (in garden) 1865. Red brick platform walls 1865.

Up platform new 1949, concrete construction, with concrete passenger shelter.

Signal Box 1888, GER Type 7 box, bricked up, disused, windows boarded up. 21-lever Saxby & Farmer 1888 patent Duplex frame (1888).

Footbridge, concrete, 1949.

LOUGHTON - ONGAR LINE '1865' BRIDGES

The original bridges on this line comprised:
- Single span overbridge, fishbelly girder 714
- Three arch overbridge, segmental arches 705, 706, 710, 712
- Three span overbridge, cast iron girders on brick pillars 701, 707
- Single arch underbridge, segmental arch 697, 703, 715
- Single arch underbridge, semicircular arch 711
- Single span underbridge, iron girder 695 (Roding Rd), 698 (Rectory Rd), 708 (Coopersale Common), 709 (Kiln Lane)
- Viaducts, semicircular arches 700, 717.

The original iron girder underbridges have all been replaced. The other original bridges survive and are described individually here and in the Gazetteer.

There are no single arch overbridges of the type found in good numbers on the Bishops Stortford – Braintree line (p.122) and the Sudbury - Shelford - Bury lines. This is no doubt a reflection of the Ongar line cuttings being too wide.

top left
The original (down) side of Alderton Hall Lane Bridge 697, which remains in near-original state.

top right
The Debden viaduct (Bridge 700), down side. The undersides of the arches on the 1865 portion were rendered in the late C20. Some of the piers have been widened and faced in engineering brick.

second left
The south side of 'Cattle Bridge' 701. The brickwork is mixed red and yellow and it is difficult to tell which is original.

third left
The west side of Bridge 703, i.e. the 1891 widening side. This has a five-ring arch although the original side of the bridge has a six-ring arch! The parapet wall and wing walls on this side have Hamblet blue brick copings which were presumably reused from the original walling on this side.

bottom left
Blake Hall Road overbridge 712. This has five-ring arches, a four-course string course, and is noticeably cambered as the road rises to the bridge on both sides. *Alan D. Simpson*

bottom right
Whilst most of the Ongar line bridges have the Hamblet double-bullnose coping bricks (see p.123), Bridges 701 and 707 have these smaller single-ended coping bricks. A few do have Hamblet markings to confirm their origin. (Photo Bridge 707).

BRIDGE 710/o104, overbridge, Ongar Park Lodge, GR 506037. 1865, red brick, three arches.

BRIDGE 711/o105, underbridge, Ongar Park Hall, GR 513037. 1865, high 12ft3in span semicircular arch.

BLAKE HALL

Main building '1865' 'small' type, 1865, red brick with white brick dressings. Photos pp. 21/22. Now a private house; visible from road. The front of the single storey portion was demolished by vandals with a bulldozer in 1987 and had to be rebuilt afterwards; although done in the correct style, the windows and door are differently positioned.

[Station platform, Gents, and Scullery demolished].

BRIDGE 712/o107, overbridge, Blake Hall Road, GR 523038. 1865, red brick, three segmental arches 22ft3in/25ft/22ft3in. Also GER wall in red brick along west side of road between this bridge and the former station road entrance.

BRIDGE 714/o110, overbridge, Pensons Hall Lane, GR 538037. 1865, yellow brick, 25ft span fishbelly girder with curving panelled brickwork above.

BRIDGE 715/o111, underbridge, footpath, GR 545035. 1865, yellow brick, low 12ft span segmental arch.

BRIDGE 717/o112, CRIPSEY BROOK VIADUCT, GR 548035. 1865, five 20ft span semicircular arches, originally yellow brick (?), much repaired and strengthened. Largely invisible owing to tree growth.

ONGAR

Main building '1865' 'large' type, 1865, red brick with white brick dressings. See p.23. Scullery (in garden) 1865.

Footwarmer House, red brick, gabled, 1896.

Porters' Room, in quasi-'1865' style, red brick with white brick dressings, hipped, 1887?

Cottages in Banson's Way – Nos 7/9/11/13 on south side 1892, Nos 2/4/6/8/10/12/14 on north side 1912.

The 1912 Ongar cottages are the best-preserved GER terrace in Essex. They are to the 1911-15 design illustrated at p.52 bottom.

The 1892 cottages at Ongar are to the same design as the Debden cottages illustrated at p.51.

Two timber-built coal merchants' office huts (c1880s) next to the goods yard entrance gate on the main road are listed as part of the station, but whilst these are on GER land they would probably not have been GER-built.

Further Reading on stations Epping to Ongar - Great Eastern in Town and Country Vol.3.

3. [SHENFIELD] TO SOUTHEND VICTORIA

BRIDGE 745, underbridge, occupation and stream, GR 637960. 1887/8, 11ft5in span segmental arch, plus 5ft span arch for stream. Photo p.99.

BRIDGE 749, overbridge, GR 658954. 1887/8, red brick, was three segmental arches but centre arch replaced by concrete span 1956. Side arches 20ft span.

BILLERICAY

Main building at street level (actually two-storey), platform buildings, and platform canopies all 1887/8, fully extant. (NB – this station is NOT of the New Essex lines type). Main building has steeply-pitched hipped roof, and large segmental-arched windows, of similar ambience to Buckhurst Hill, but frontage defaced c1960 by addition of crude flat-roof Parcels Office extension (now café). Platform buildings have segmental-arched windows (unlike stations beyond). For platform canopies see p.45. Valancing (MkII standard) removed pre-1950s. New footbridge 1994.

Further Reading – GE Journal 127.

BRIDGE 754, overbridge, High Street/Stock Road, GR 675949. 1887/8, faced in engineering brick, three 25ft span semicircular arches, 31ft 3in high. Panelled parapet walls.

BRIDGE 755, overbridge, Norsey Road, GR 677949. 1887/8, faced in engineering brick, four 25ft span semicircular arches, skew, 46ft8in high. Panelled parapet walls. The most substantial road bridge on the New Essex lines.

BRIDGE 760, overbridge, occupation, Claypitts Hill Wood, GR 706945. 1887/8, faced in engineering brick, three 25ft span semicircular arches, skew, 26ft4in high.

RAMSDEN BELLHOUSE. One pair of standard New Essex lines cottages, 1888, much altered. (On west side of Church Road immediately north of line).

WICKFORD

Main building/house (down side) 1887/8, with New Essex lines features but not to any of the common plans used for stations beyond Wickford. Small c1960 extension east end. New entrance / enlarged Booking Hall 1981.

Continued on p.97

MORE ON '1865' STATION BUILDINGS IN ESSEX

(following on from pp.21-24)

'1865' station buildings, whilst very standardised in their architectural features, reveal more variations in their constructional details the more one looks at them.

The use of different coloured bricks (and of painted stucco surrounds on the Bishops Stortford – Braintree line) have been referred to already; it is perhaps surprising that the red brick with white brick dressings version was not more generally employed, as it is decidedly more visually satisfying.

Another principal cause of differences is the use of bricks of different dimensions (and different thicknesses of mortar). If one takes the 'small' type stations in Essex, the number of courses between the plinth top and the eaves varies from 65 at Debden to 72 at Rayne (3.3 inches per course to 3.0 inches per course). The main visible effect of this is in relation to the quoins which are differently arranged in every case (except that Takeley and Felsted are the same in all brick coursing matters – even though they are built of different bricks). The quoins are normally of four courses, although there are some threes and fives. The varying relationship between the quoins and the upper and lower string courses (which are always of two courses) is particularly noticeable. However, there are also other variations which go beyond anything caused by differing bricks, and seem to be quite gratuitous; e.g. at Takeley and Felsted there are five courses between the string courses, and three courses between the upper string course and the first floor window cills, whereas the corresponding figures at Rayne are four and six. More surprisingly still, these differences sometimes also involve significant dimensional differences in the relative positioning of the windows etc. In the cases just mentioned, the cills of the first floor windows at Rayne are 8in further from the head of the ground floor windows than at Takeley/Felsted. It is difficult to believe that any good reasons could have existed for such differences to have been purposely specified, which leaves one wondering on whose decision they were determined.

At all stations the arrangement of the brick coursing etc on the platform side is the same as on the road side.

The house section of the building at 'medium' and 'large' stations is taller than at 'small' stations. The number of courses between plinth and eaves varies from 73 at Epping to 85 at Theydon Bois. The ground floor windows in the house section at these stations are both wider and deeper than the corresponding windows at 'small' stations; they match the windows in the pavilion at the other end.

The 'handing' of the '1865' station buildings in Essex is as follows ('right' means the house section is at the right-hand end as viewed from the road side)

Loughton R (p.96)
Debden R (p.91)
Theydon Bois R (p.22)
Epping L (p.95)
North Weald L (p.95)
Blake Hall L (pp. 21/22)
Ongar R (p.23)
Takeley R (p.94)
Dunmow R (p.95)
Felsted L (p.94)
Rayne R (pp. 22/94)
Braintree L (p.96)
Marks Tey L (p.96)

top left
Takeley after its 2006 restoration by Essex County Council. It had previously been boarded-up and derelict for many years.

middle left
Felsted station is excellently preserved in private hands.

bottom left
Rayne's house extension does not form quite such a satisfactory composition on the road side, not helped by the lack of a ground floor window. As at Epping, though, an effort was made to match the brick colour.

right
This 1930s view of Epping shows the 1865 'large' single-storey up platform block before it was altered, as well as the arrangement of the glazed covered area on the platform side of the main building at 'large' and 'medium' stations. At right, under the ivy, is the c1890 Station Master's Office.

top right
North Weald road side in the 1980s. This station features an unusually high plinth on the road side (and a low plinth on the platform side) because of the ground falling away. Another odd feature at North Weald is that there are four courses of proud brickwork under the eaves instead of the usual two. (However Blake Hall has three courses and Ongar only one!).

Alan D. Simpson

second right
The '1865' single-storey up platform block at Dunmow (now demolished). These 'other platform' blocks at 'medium' stations are shorter than those at 'large' stations, *cf* the view of Epping below. The left hand section of the glazed screen had been taken out by the date of this photograph (1968). Behind is the large goods shed, of the standard type used on the '1865' lines; none of these now survive in Essex.

J.E. Connor

below
Another 1968 view of Dunmow, showing the platform side arrangement of an 1865 'medium' size station. Again the glazed waiting area is shorter than at the 'large' stations. (All now demolished).

J.E. Connor

third right
When the Station Master's house at Epping was extended (left) in 1891, everything was done in proper '1865' style, and a good matching red brick was also found.

top

Marks Tey in the 1920s – the 1864-built 'large' type main building on the up side, demolished in the early 1970s after incurable sewerage problems came to light. As at Braintree, an additional bedroom had been provided above the central section in the late GER period. Note that the central section of 'large' buildings was symmetrical on the road side; the 'medium' buildings omitted one of the large windows here and in consequence had a non-symmetrical central section.

Graham Austin collection.

middle

Loughton in the Edwardian years. Like Marks Tey this was built wholly in white brick. The whole of the 1865 station was demolished soon (exact date not known) after the 1940 station opened.

Alan D. Simpson collection.

bottom

Braintree in 1982, showing the 1886 scullery block at left. The house section had already been rendered in late GER views.

top left

A closer view of the iron brackets used on the platform side of the 'small' stations (Rayne).

top right

Detail of the brickwork in the 'pavilion' section at Theydon Bois. It should be noted that the dimensions and relative positions of the arch and 'keystone' of the ground floor windows, and the string course, are quite different at the stations on this line when compared with the stucco surrounds on the Bishops Stortford – Braintree line.

bottom right

The 1865 scullery block at Rayne. It is to virtually the same design as those on the Ongar line. At right is the later WC/coal store against the west wall of the house extension.

Upper floor of Station Master's house section demolished 1998 after fire. [House was of the Rayleigh-Burnham type but had a 'striped' (vice tile-hung) gable on the road side].

Down platform canopy 1888, same design as Billericay, cut back in width and valancing removed 1955, new roofing 1980s.

Up platform buildings and flat canopy 1978.

Footbridge 1888, lattice, altered 1955 (see photo and note p.49).

BRIDGE 770, underbridge, River Crouch, GR 748935. 1888, faced in engineering brick, 20ft span six-ring skew arch 'tunnel'.

WICK LANE. One pair of cottages (Nos 59/61, on east side of road immediately south of Southminster line bridge). Gabled, but original design uncertain owing to extreme alterations. Probably 1912.

[The other GER cottages in Wick Lane, and the crossing house, are demolished].

BRIDGE 772, overbridge, GR 767919. 1888, faced in engineering brick, was three segmental skew arches but centre arch replaced by concrete span 1955. Side arches reinforced with concrete.

RAYLEIGH

Main building/house (up side), down platform buildings, and platform canopies all 1888/9. For details see p.32. c1960 the original Gents and lock-up at the west end of the up side buildings were demolished and a new extension erected with toilets and staff accommodation. Also c1960 the original road side entrance doorway in the 'pavilion' became a window, and a new entrance doorway was made to the east of this, with a small flat canopy.

'Standard' canopies, all on columns, with quarter-circle longitudinal brackets. Cut back in width and valancing removed 1955.

Footbridge 1889, lattice, altered 1955 (see note p.49). Extra staircase to east added on down side 1964.

[Cottages and Goods Shed demolished].

Further Reading – GE Journal 118.

BRIDGE 779, overbridge, footpath, GR 829931. 1888, faced in engineering brick, originally three segmental arches, 19ft high.

HOCKLEY

Main building (up side), down platform buildings, and platform canopies all 1888/9. For details see p.34. Small c1960 extensions at both ends of up side buildings, and west end of down side buildings.

'Standard' canopies, all on columns, with quarter-circle longitudinal brackets. Cut back in width and valancing removed 1955.

Footbridge 1889, lattice, altered 1955 (see note p.49).

Hipped-roof Goods Lock-up, 1889 (photo p.34).

[Station Master's house and cottages demolished].

HAWKWELL SIDING. One pair of standard New Essex lines cottages, 1888/9, badly altered. (South of line at GR 862919).

ROCHFORD

Main building/house (down side), up platform buildings, and platform canopies all 1888/9. For details see p.33. Small c1960 extension at north end of down side buildings. Also c1960 the original road side entrance doorway in the 'pavilion' became a window, and a new entrance doorway was made to the north of this, with a small flat canopy.

'Standard' canopies, all on columns, with quarter-circle longitudinal brackets. Cut back in width and valancing removed 1955.

Footbridge 1889, lattice, altered 1955 (see note p.49).

Hipped-roof Goods Lock-up 1888/9 (at north end of down side buildings).

Goods Shed 1889, converted c1983 to The Freight House public hall.

One pair of standard New Essex lines cottages, 1888/9 (photo p.51).

Terrace of four gabled cottages, 1912 (photo p.52). Contract to J.Eglin 6.6.1912 at £820.

MORE ON STANDARD 'NEW LINES' COTTAGES

top left

A close view of the standard design of front door canopy used on the Essex New Lines cottages and some (not all) of the Station Master's houses. This is the SM's house section at Burnham-on-Crouch.

top right

This one cottage (out of the six) at Woodham Ferrers remains unspoilt.

Whilst we refer to these New Lines cottages as 'standard', there are as usual more differences to be found the more one looks! For example, the Woodham Ferrers cottages have four courses of ordinary brickwork between the head of the ground floor window and the two-course 'string course'. The Prittlewell cottages have only one intermediate course, the Rochford (p.51) and Southminster cottages have two courses, and the Cold Norton cottages have three! This reflects/produces noticeable differences in the relative positions of the windows, door canopies, etc.

bottom right

This is the only one of the four 1889 cottages at Prittlewell to remain in original condition.

bottom left

The cottages in Hall Road, Southminster, are comparatively unspoilt.

ROCHFORD RESERVOIR. GER reservoir constructed 1904/5 for loco water supply at Southend. Capacity 6 million gallons. Now in a park open to public (west side of Southend Road, GR 876902).

PRITTLEWELL

Main building (up side), and platform canopies, 1888/9. [Buildings behind down platform demolished 1964].

'Standard' canopies, all on columns, with quarter-circle longitudinal brackets. Cut back in width and valancing removed 1955.

Footbridge 1889, lattice, altered 1955 (see note p.49).

Electric substation 1955 (west side, south of station building).

Two pairs of standard New Essex lines cottages, 1889. (North side of East Street, east of railway bridge).

Terrace of six cottages, 1892, same design as the 1891 Chappel cottages. Contract to Allen Fairhead Snr & Jnr of Enfield 5.7.1892 at £1,250. (To east of 1889 cottages). Plans, including elevations, exist at ERO, ref. D/Z 346/3144.

Terrace of six cottages (Station Terrace) 1915, all badly altered. Unique plain gabled design with front doors recessed behind semicircular arches.

[Goods Lock-up and Station Master's house demolished].

Further Reading – GE Journal 100.

SOUTHEND VICTORIA

Main buildings 1888/9, see pp. 34/35 for details. [The main losses are the removal of the porte-cochere on the west side and the large covered area over the roadway on the east side].

Platform buildings behind stops end of platform 2 new/altered late C20.

Platform canopies on both island platforms 1889, see p.47, new roofing 1980s.

Signal Box 1889, GER Type 8 box, derelict, no frame.

Further Reading – British Railways Illustrated Vol.16 No.9 (June 2007): 1930s photosurvey with buildings still in original condition.

Bridge 745 makes a pleasant little composition. It is now accessible, in Hutton Country Park. *Nigel Bowdidge*

The south end of Rochford Goods Shed in its current guise. It is to the same arrangement as Maldon West (p.66) but is a taller building, hence the extra windows. The right hand arch was the former rail access.

The Prittlewell 1892 cottages, all rewindowed and retiled but otherwise comparatively intact.

Detail of the Booking Office pavilion canopies' struts at Wickford (left) and Hockley (below) (see also Rayleigh p.33).

4. [WICKFORD] TO SOUTHMINSTER

BRIDGE 798, overbridge, Wick Lane, GR 753931. 1888/9, faced in engineering brick, three 25ft6in segmental arches, slightly skew.

BRIDGE 800, underbridge, River Crouch, GR 767941. 1888/9, faced in engineering brick, three arches 10ft/22ft/10ft, skew. Repaired and strengthened 1963.

BATTLESBRIDGE

[Station buildings – photo p.140 - and Goods Shed demolished].

Station Master's House, 1889, see p.53.

'The Bungalow', built (c1909?) by John Wilson on GER land, between SM's house and the railway embankment, as a country retreat, subsequently let to railway staff until sold 1958.

BRIDGE 807, underbridge, stream/flood opening, GR 798975. 1888/9, faced in engineering brick, two segmental arches 25ft7in and 15ft1in, skew
(and similar bridge 809 at GR 799975).

WOODHAM FERRERS

[Main station building (down side) demolished except for a small portion now scarcely recognisable. For photo when intact see p.139].

Two bays only of 1889 'standard' down platform canopy, on columns with quarter-circle longitudinal brackets, cut back in width 1985, original valancing remains.

Disused up platform still in situ [buildings demolished].

[Footbridge demolished].

Three pairs of standard New Essex lines cottages, 1889 (p.98).

HOGWELL (GR 826978). One pair of standard New Essex lines cottages, 1889.

FAMBRIDGE

[All 1889 station buildings demolished].

Footbridge, steel, 1985.

Three pairs of standard New Essex lines cottages, 1889, mostly badly altered.

[Station Master's house demolished].

ALTHORNE

[All 1889 station buildings demolished. For photo see p.140].

Station Master's house, 1889, rewindowed but otherwise in good condition.

Two pairs of standard New Essex lines cottages, 1889.

Further Reading – GE Journal 126.

BRIDGE 824, underbridge, occupation, GR925968. 1888/9, faced in engineering brick, 14ft8in span arch.

BURNHAM-ON-CROUCH

Station Master's house section and part only of the rest of main (up side) building of 1889 remain, to be restored. (See p.32).

Three bays only of 1889 'standard' canopy on up platform, on columns, with quarter-circle longitudinal brackets (photo p.46), cut back in width 1985, original valancing remains.

Disused down platform still in situ [buildings demolished].

[Goods Shed and cottages demolished].

SOUTHMINSTER

Station Master's house section and part only of the rest of main building of 1889 remain. Photos p.33 and p.139. Recently restored but with incorrect pattern sashes.

Three bays only of 1889 'standard' canopy, on columns, with quarter-circle longitudinal brackets, cut back in width 1985, original valancing remains.

Two pairs of standard New Essex lines cottages, 1889 (in Hall Road). Photo p.98. [Third pair, in Station Yard, demolished].

[Goods Shed demolished].

Further Reading – GE Journal 102.

below right Althorne in its heyday. At left are the now-demolished station buildings, for which see the closer view at p.140. At right the east front of the detached Station Master's house, which is very similar to the corresponding front at Wivenhoe (p.30), although the gable here is lower-pitched. *Nigel Bowdidge collection*

below left A recent view of the south front of Althorne Station Master's house (which is in good condition but has been rewindowed). This front is noticeably different from the corresponding (NW) front at Wivenhoe. Althorne also has specially carved struts to the door canopy, like the New Essex lines station buildings, instead of a 'standard' cottage type canopy. The house at Cold Norton is very much as Althorne.

The Battlesbridge house (p.53) is quite similar to Althorne but not identical, e.g. at Battlesbridge the door canopy extends above the string course, and the windows are differently positioned, and the gable more steeply-pitched.

Bridge 824. The brick coursing in the left hand spandrel is very defective.

Bridge 839 has 'panelled' brickwork in the parapet wall, as do most of the New Essex lines bridges. As at many bridges on these lines the stretchers here show a more pinkish hue than the headers, creating a strong 'striped' impression in some lights.

5. [WOODHAM FERRERS] TO [MALDON EAST]

Current Status of Trackbed

Woodham Ferrers Jn to King Edward's Rd (GR 812979)	Eliminated
King Edward's Rd to B1012 Burnham Rd (GR 815982)	Intact, walkable in part, overgrown
B1012 to Woodham Rd (GR 820987)	Eliminated
Woodham Rd to GR 824989	Cutting/embankment intact, no access
GR 824989 to St Stephen's Rd (GR 847999)	Intact, Public Bridleway, walkable
St Stephen's Rd to Latchingdon Rd (GR 849004)	Cutting intact, no access
Cold Norton station site	Built on
GR 851006 to GR 849015	Traceable as boundaries, no access
GR 849015 to Purleigh Street (GR 848021)	Embankment intact, no access
Purleigh Street to Baron's Lane (GR 846025)	Traceable as field boundary
Baron's Lane to GR 843044	Track, private
GR 843044 to N. of Limebrook Way (GR 842097)	Intact, nature reserve, free access, walkable
Maldon West goods yard to S. end of tunnel (GR 842063)	Industrial Estate, accessible
Spital Road (GR 824064) to Maldon E. Jn (GR 849078)	Converted to road
Maldon West Jn to Langford Jn curve	Embankment intact

BRIDGE 833, overbridge, Woodham Road, GR 820987. 1889, faced in engineering brick, three segmental arches 27ft7in/25ft6in/25ft7in, skew. Northern arch distorted.

BRIDGE 835, underbridge, occupation, GR 831991. 1889, faced in engineering brick, segmental arch, 10ft span.

BRIDGE 836, overbridge, Church Lane (Stow Maries), GR 835992. 1889, faced in engineering brick, three segmental arches all of 25ft6in span.

BRIDGE 839, overbridge, St Stephen's Road, GR 847999. 1889, 25ft6in girder span, wrought iron girders with brick jack arching, abutments and parapet walls faced in engineering brick.

BRIDGE 840, overbridge, Latchingdon Road, GR 849004. 1889, faced in engineering brick, three segmental arches all of 25ft6in span.

[Bridges 833, 836 and 840 represent a standard design of overbridge used on the New Essex lines, see article in GE Journal 103 which includes a detailed drawing of Bridge 836. All three bridges are accessible but unfortunately scarcely appreciable owing to mass tree growth].

COLD NORTON

Station Master's house, 1889, similar to Althorne.

Two pairs of standard New Essex lines cottages, 1889, all much altered.

[Station buildings and platform demolished. For photo see p.140].

MALDON WEST

Goods Shed, 1889, see p.66.

Two pairs of standard New Essex lines cottages, 1889 (photos p.51 and p.102). No.107 recently extended in original style.

GER boundary wall 1889 in engineering brick along main road between these cottages.

[Station buildings (photo p.141), platforms, and Station Master's house demolished].

BRIDGE 849, Maldon West tunnel, GR 842063. 29ft span at rail level. 204ft long. South portal extant. This is an artificial tunnel to avoid a very skew bridge.

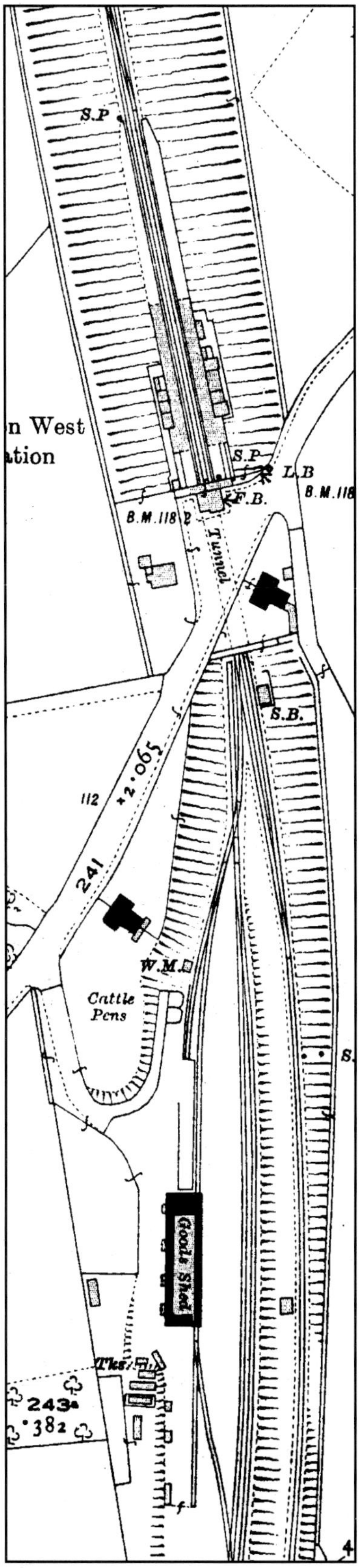

The southern pair of GER cottages at Maldon West. In contrast to the damage done to these houses elswhere, here the owner of the right hand cottage has built an extension in proper original style. In front is the continuation of the GER engineering brick wall seen also at p.51.

left

Maldon West 1919 survey Ordnance Survey. Buildings surviving in 2006 shaded black. The present roundabout occupies the site of the station platforms.

bottom left

Cold Norton 1919 survey Ordnance Survey. Buildings extant in 2006 shaded black.

right

Wickham Bishops viaducts and station, 1920 survey Ordnance Survey. This copy of the map has been amended in pencil (by its original owner) to show how the northern end of the Mill Stream viaduct was replaced by embankment under the LNER. Originally 543ft long with 26 spans, it was reduced to a length of 150ft (10 spans). The map also shows clearly how the post-1854 single line over the viaducts was the former up line of 1848-54. The viaducts are now 20ft 2in wide but the original width was approx. 32ft 6in.

There were originally six timber viaducts between Witham and Maldon, the other four (now removed) being

Bridge 871 at Blackwater Lane, Witham, 165ft long (12 spans).

Bridge 858 over the Chelmer Navigation at Maldon, 125ft long (9 spans).

Bridge 857 at Maldon, a flood opening immediately SE of Bridge 858, 73ft long (6 spans).

Bridge 856, an adjacent flood opening on the coal siding line, 75ft long (6 spans).

There were no timber viaducts on the Witham – Braintree section.

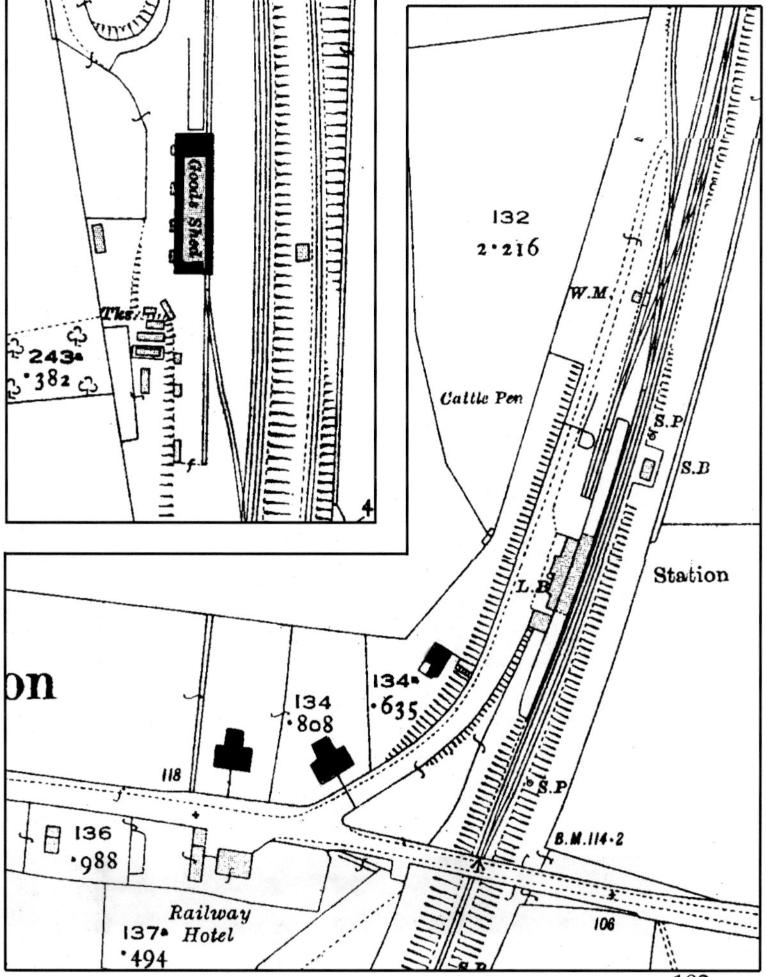

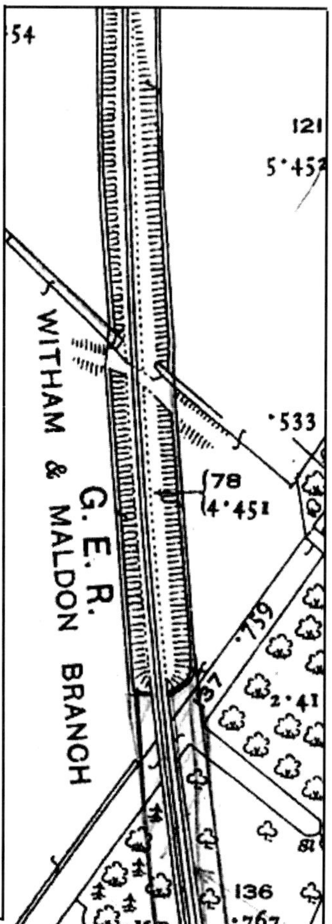

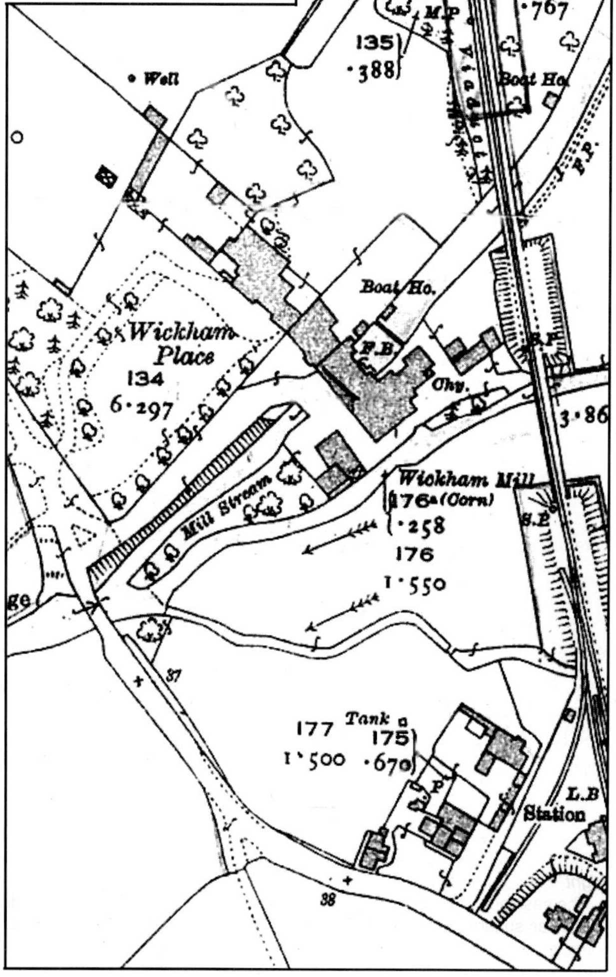

6. [WITHAM] TO MALDON EAST

Current Status of Trackbed

Witham Jn to Colchester Rd (GR 825151)	Eliminated (absorbed into industrial area)
Colchester Rd to Blue Mills Rd (GR 824131)	Intact, footpath owned by ECC, walkable *except* from GR 826148 to GR 826144 the path is beside the formation on the east side not on the formation, and the timber viaduct at GR 825159 has been removed so that it is necessary to divert via Blackwater Lane, Maldon Rd, and footpath north of Constance Close to regain the formation.
Blue Mills Rd to N. end of Wickham Bishops station	Largely intact but no access
Wickham Bishops station site	Intact, private
Station Rd (GR 824115) to Bridge 864 at old church (GR 826113)	Intact, no access
Bridge 864 to Witham Rd (GR 837095)	Intact, footpath owned by ECC, walkable
Witham Rd to GR 838092	Eliminated
GR 838092 to Maldon Rd (GR 841089)	Semi-intact, no access
Maldon Rd to GR 848081	Intact, footpath, walkable
GR 848081 to former LC at The Causeway (GR 852076)	Converted to roads
The Causeway to end of branch	Eliminated, absorbed into industrial sites

BRIDGE 872, overbridge, Colchester Road ('Catholic Bridge'), GR 825151. 1847/8. Yellow brick abutments, cast iron girder span.

BRIDGE 868, underbridge, Wickham Bishops Mill Stream Viaduct, GR 824118. See p.13 and map here for details.

BRIDGE 867, underbridge, Wickham Bishops River Viaduct, GR 824117. See p.13 and map here for details.

WICKHAM BISHOPS

Station House, 1848, see p.12. Now much altered and extended. No access.

Platform, late C19. No access.

BRIDGE 865, overbridge, Station Road, GR 824115. 1847/8. Yellow brick, 25ft10in span cast iron girder main span, two 10ft span semicircular arches either side.

BRIDGE 864, overbridge, GR 826113. 1847/8. Yellow brick, three segmental arches, centre span 26ft, side spans 20ft.

LANGFORD

Station House (now 'Railway Cottage'), C18 house purchased by ECR. Photo p.104.

Platform, late C19/early C20.

MALDON EAST

Station building, 1847/8, see pp.13 and 104, now used as offices.

Portion of 1890/1 'standard' canopy.

Goods Shed, 1848 (photo inside front cover).

Small portion only of Loco Shed, 1848.

[At 51 High St Maldon, formerly Post Office now Dorothy Perkins, the rear part of the shop has two columns from the pre-1906 Witham station platform canopies. Probably 1879. See drawing in GE Journal 38 p.23].

above

Bridge 872, one of the Witham – Maldon line's four 1847/8 cast iron girder bridges with brick jack arching. The other three were Bridge 869 at Blue Mills (demolished 1971), Bridge 865 at Wickham Bishops (photo below), and Bridge 859 at Langford (photo at GE Journal 96.19 – now filled in).

Bridge 872 suffered from having to carry the heavy A12 traffic until the Witham bypass opened in 1964. Drawings for supporting steelwork were prepared in 1941, but the present steel supports were of course only installed after closure of this section of the line in 1977. The red brickwork infilling in the outer face of the girders (also found at Bridge 859) was not an original feature. Photo 2001.

right

The east face of Bridge 865 (2001). This bridge is in largely original condition but it too has suffered from structural weaknesses. Note that this bridge has a course of blue bricks immediately above the girder where Bridge 872 has a stone course.

top

An unusual montage view of Langford from Bridge 859 showing the C18 station house (which remains unaltered today, save for the brickwork of the frontage being painted white).
Photographer unknown - Allen Chaplin collection.

middle

Maldon East in all its glory in the late GER period. The most noticeable difference today is the removal of all the stone finials of which there were 14 on the balcony (still there in the 1970s) and no less than 42 on the roofline (removed at an earlier date).

The 1848 platform canopy (for which see view in Swindale, *Branch Lines to Maldon*) was of an exuberance almost unparalleled in this country. In 1890/1 the platform was widened and the replacement 'standard' canopy provided.
The Lens of Sutton collection

left

Cressing in June 1954, when the station house was still in original condition (*cf* Wickham Bishops p.12). By the 1970s it had been plastered, and subsequent changes have left it unrecognisable. The (top half of the) 1891 GER Type 7 signal box is now at the Colne Valley Railway site.
Gordon Biddle

right
The 1848 White Notley crossing house in the 1960s. The front left section with the lean-to roof was a later extension. The main recent changes are the removal of two of the chimneys, the removal of the ridge tiles, and the installing of modern window frames.
The ridge tiles are the same as those at Wickham Bishops (p.12), and the steeply pitched roofs are also a common feature.
G.L.Pring / Railway Record of the British Isles

7. [WITHAM] TO BRAINTREE

BRIDGE 2106, overbridge, Braintree Road, GR 819157. 1847/8, yellow brick, three segmental arches 20ft6in/25ft9in/20ft6in span. Widened on NW side, concrete span, late C20.

CHERRY TREE CROSSING (GR 814161). Crossing house, 1891.

BRIDGE 2105, underbridge, Hole Farm, GR 803177. 1847/8, yellow brick, segmental arch, 11ft9in span.

BRIDGE 2104, underbridge, 'Blyth's Bridge', occupation, GR 799181. 9ft9in span brick arch. No access.

WHITE NOTLEY

Small Booking Office/Signal Box building, 1977, boarded up/disused.
Crossing House, 1848, altered late C20.

BRIDGE 2103, underbridge, occupation, GR 786191. 1847/8, yellow brick, 12ft3in span horseshoe arch 'tunnel'.

CRESSING

Waiting Room/B.O. building 1892, with canopy (Mk I 'standard' valancing).
Station House, 1848. Very badly altered and extended late C20.

BRAINTREE FREEPORT

(No buildings except a small shelter).

BRAINTREE

Station building, '1865' large type, 1865/6, red brick with white brick dressings. Photo p.96. Original Booking Office screen (as per Ongar, p.23). House section rendered. Additional bedroom 1900 above central section. Scullery, with hipped roof, added on east side of house 1886/7 in quasi-'1865' style.
Platform canopy 1886/7 (see p.45).
Footwarmer House 1899 (see p.67).
Two cottages, 1911 (contract to Clark & Sons June 1911 at £398). Of the 1911-15 type (see p.52).
[Goods yard now redeveloped – nothing remains. For 1848 station building see p.135].

left
Closer view of the Mk I 'standard' valancing on the 1892 Cressing Waiting Room / B.O. building's canopy. Photo 1972.

below
Bridge 2103 from the south west. This horseshoe-arch 'tunnel' has a length of 61ft.

8. [KELVEDON] TO TOLLESBURY PIER

Owing to its 'Light Railway' construction, there are no remains of the stations and few other remains from this line, and most of the trackbed has been eliminated. The most significant extant section is from near Tolleshunt Knights church (GR 927138) to Old Hall (GR 950117), which survives as private roads. The trackbed from Wycke Lane (GR 966098) to the sea wall at Tollesbury Pier is also extant.

BRIDGE 875, overbridge, Blind Lane, GR 917145. This was the line's only overbridge. 1904, 25ft 4in girder span plus 16ft span brick arch, all now filled in and only the parapet walls visible.

TOLLESHUNT D'ARCY

One cottage, 1912. Of the 1911-15 type (p.52), much altered and extended. Contract to M.Richards & Son of Witham, June 1912, at £255. Plans exist at ERO ref. D/RMa/Pb3/84.

TOLLESBURY PIER

There are no remains of the pier itself but portions of the angled timber palisading that protected the foot of the embankment on the inner section of the pier are still in situ.

[For the demolished station building see photo p.142].

Further Reading – P. Paye, The Tollesbury Branch, OPC 1985.

The 1912 cottage at Tolleshunt D'Arcy soon after its construction, looking south across the level crossing.

The fireplace in the Goods Shed office at Chappel. The central portion is as per the Booking Office fireplace (p.38), but the sections either side are much narrower. The Station Master's office also has a fireplace. However the full story of the design variations in these fireplaces remains to be written!

9. SUDBURY LINE, [MARKS TEY] TO NORTH OF BURES

Crossing House at GR907250. 1849?, much altered but appears to be similar to the crossing house at Cornard.

BRIDGE 879, overbridge, occupation, GR 903254. 1848/9, red brick with white brick dressings, 30ft span three-centred arch, skew.

BRIDGE 880, overbridge, occupation, GR 904257. 1848/9, yellowy-red brick, 30ft span three-centred arch.

BRIDGE 881, overbridge, Moor Road / Tey Road, GR 898263. 1848/9, red brick with white brick dressings, 63ft4in span 'flying' segmental arch (photo p.15).

BRIDGE 882, overbridge, Bacons Lane, GR 897271. 1848/9, red brick, 30ft span three-centred arch, skew.

BRIDGE 883, underbridge, Popes Road, GR 896277. 1848/9, red brick, 11ft10in span semicircular-arch 'tunnel'.

BRIDGE 884, CHAPPEL VIADUCT – see p.15.

CHAPPEL & WAKES COLNE

(see pp.36-39 for more information and photographs).

Station House, EUR, c1850, with 1880s single storey extensions.
Two storey platform buildings to south of House, 1850s-80s.
Main station building and platform canopy 1891.
Coal shed (formerly stables), c1860s, derelict.
Goods Shed with office, 1891.
'Traffic Office', brick hut, c1880s.
Signal Box, 1892, GER Type 7 box, 38-lever Saxby & Farmer 1888 pattern Duplex frame (1892).
Four cottages, 1891.
'Sunderland Arms' later 'Railway Tavern' public house, built c1860 on railway land, circumstances of building unknown.

plus buildings from elsewhere re-erected here by East Anglian Railway Museum

Chappel North signal box, ex Mistley, GER Type 3 box, 1882, 27-lever McKenzie & Holland 1873 patent frame (from Mistley, 1882). Photo p.68. Chappel South signal box, ex Fotherby, GNR timber hut, 1886, fitted with 16-lever Stevens-made Stevens frame from Beckton Gas Works.
Footbridge, ex Sudbury, 1887 there. Photo p.48.
Cast iron Urinal ex Cockfield.
Smith's bookstall ex North Harrow, 1936 there (in Booking Hall).
Crane (outside), Kirkstall Forge Co. 1865. [See note in Corrigenda].
Crane (inside Goods Shed), ex Saffron Walden.
Water crane, ex Dunmow.

BRIDGE 886, overbridge, Spring Gardens Road, GR 898291. 1848/9, red brick with white brick dressings, 30ft span three-centred arch.

Bridge 883 from the west.

Bridge 891.

BRIDGE 887, overbridge, GR 901299. 1848/9, red brick, 30ft span three-centred arch.

BRIDGE 888, overbridge, GR 907313. 1848/9, red brick with white brick dressings, 30ft span three-centred arch.

MOUNT BURES CROSSING. Crossing House, 1849 (see p.53).

BURES

The only surviving structure is a timber hut, date not known but pre-1920s.

[For the demolished station building see photos cover / p.136].

BRIDGE 891, underbridge, Station Hill, GR 903339. 1848/9, red brick, 25ft span segmental arch.

BRIDGE 892, overbridge, occupation, GR 899348. 1848/9, 20ft brick arch. No access.

BRIDGE 897, underbridge, River Stour ('Pitmore Viaduct'), GR 891369. On county boundary. Rebuilt 1903. Girder span over river, on brick piers. Flood channel spans either side.

---

10. [COLCHESTER] TO WALTON-ON-NAZE

BRIDGE 1001, underbridge, footpath, GR 004263. 1846/7 ? Red brick skew arch.

EAST GATE JUNCTION SIGNAL BOX. LNER, 1924, special design. 35-lever McKenzie & Holland frame. Photo p.108.

HYTHE

Station building/house THR standard type, 1863, red brick with gault brick dressings, derelict. Covered area on platform side infilled with brick 1989. Single storey extension with flat roof at east end 1918 (Booking Office). [1863 single storey portions at west end demolished].

Down platform shelter 1989.

Coal Hopper shed in up sidings, 1966, derelict.

Further Reading – GE Journals 112, 121, 125.

BRIDGE 1009, underbridge, Hythe Tramway bridge over River Colne, GR 014248. Largely a 1960 reconstruction. Disused.

WIVENHOE

Station building/Station Master's house/up platform canopy 1886, see pp.30-31 for details, also p.44 and p.110. Canopy reduced in length at east end; also cut back in width 1957 and valancing removed.

Footbridge 1886 (see note p.48). Contract to Cleveland Bridge & Engineering Co 16.2.1886. Replacement higher span 1960s.

Rear and one side wall only of 1886 signal box.

Goods Shed with office, 1903 (see p.66).

Stable 1903 (see p.67).

Further Reading – P. Paye, The Brightlingsea Branch, John Masters 1997.

BRIDGE 1017, overbridge, Alresford Road, GR 052215. 1866, red brick, three 26ft span segmental arches, skew. Piers have two relieving arches. Parapet walls rebuilt 1958. This is the only remaining overbridge on the THR line surviving in anything like original condition.

ALRESFORD

Station building/house THR standard type, 1865/6, red brick with gault brick dressings, upper storey now painted over. Photo p.19. Single storey portions at east end remain.

[1889 down platform Waiting Room/toilets block demolished; it was to the same design as the Great Bentley 1890 up platform block].

Footbridge, lattice, 1889, double stairways on both platforms, replacement higher span 1957. See note p.49. Contract to Eastwood Swingler & Co 5.11.1889.

Gatekeeper's hut, brick, gabled, c1900.

Further Reading – GE Journal 105.

ALRESFORD COLCHESTER ROAD CROSSING (GR 068215). Gatekeeper's hut, brick, curved roof, c1900.

THORINGTON

[Station buildings demolished. 1885 down platform building demolished 2006. For photos see p.137].

Gatekeeper's hut, 1883?, timber, gabled. Wholly reclad 1999, the only remaining original external feature is the (notched) barge-boards.

FRATING LEVEL CROSSING. Gatekeeper's hut, c1900, brick, curved roof. Disused.

East Gate Junction signal box when new in September 1924. A *Railway Magazine* article noted that 'erection of the new box was itself a problem, in that it had to be fitted into a very limited space, and it was also thought to be desirable that its architecture should harmonise to some extent with the old-fashioned buildings and houses in the vicinity. This accounts for the somewhat unusual and distinctive architecture of the box, which is in Old English (sic) style......'.

The box abuts on to an old timber-framed cottage (not visible from this angle) and is narrower at the LC end. The jettied-out section enables the signalman to see both ways along the road. The large locking room windows have now been bricked up.

Only a handful of signal boxes in the UK were ever built to special designs in this way to harmonise with surrounding buildings.

GREAT BENTLEY

Station building/house THR standard type, 1865/6, red brick with gault brick dressings, upper storey rendered. Single storey portions at east end remain. Major alterations carried out c1890 – single storey flat roofed Booking Hall added at west end, and a larger covered waiting area created on platform side by removing the west end 'pavilion' and erecting new canopy. Booking Hall has fireplace with small GER 'batswing' device.

Up platform Waiting Room/toilets block and canopy 1890, in light red brick. Canopy has Wivenhoe type columns and brackets: cut back in width and valancing removed 1957. Photo p.110.

Footbridge, lattice, 1889, double stairways on both platforms, replacement higher span 1957. See note p.49. Contract let 16.4.1889 at £422. 'Joseph Westwood & Co Millwall London E 1889' maker's plates.

Further Reading - GE Journal 111.

WEELEY

Station building/house THR standard type, 1865/6, red brick with gault brick dressings (p.19). Disused and boarded up but is in better original condition than the other surviving buildings of this type. [Single storey portions at west end demolished].

Lamp hut, red brick, gabled, derelict.
Footbridge, concrete, c1957.
[1884 up platform building demolished – see p.137].

Further Reading – GE Journal 123.

THORPE-LE-SOKEN

Station building/house THR, special design, 1866, red brick with gault brick dressings. Single storey portions at east end remain, but altered. Restored 2005. Photos p.18 and p.111.

Brick entrance gateway/cycle shed on disused down platform, 1989.

Waiting Rooms block on up island platform 1882 (contract to O.T.Gibbons 18.4.1882 at £675). Timber on brick base. Canopy supported by 'GER' wall brackets (see p.43). Photo p.111.

Staff room/store block to east of last, c1890, timber on brick base.

Signal Box 1882, GER Type 2 box, brick to floor construction. Extended at west end 1940. Now has panel (1989).
Booking Office (to west of SB), brick, 1989.
Footbridge, concrete, 1957.

Further Reading – GE Journal 80.

KIRBY CROSS

Station building/house THR standard type, 1866, red brick with gault brick dressings. [Single storey portions at west end demolished].

Up platform building/canopy 1899, boarded up. 'Large circle' type brackets. Valancing cut back slightly.

FRINTON

Main building 1887/8 (see p.31). Extended at east end (1920s?), also short flat-roof extension at west end for bookstall (1930s).

right
These c1910 and 1997 views of Great Bentley show that, whilst the down side buildings remain in the basic form to which they were altered c1890, there have as ever been a number of minor changes, *viz*
rendering of the upper storey
replacement sashes to a different pattern in the upper floor platform side window
removal of the wooden 'canopy' above this window (also on the road side)
the original semicircular-arched window in the 'pavilion' replaced by a door in the late C20
semicircular-arched door in the c1890 eastward extension to the 'pavilion' replaced by a new doorway in the late C20
additional small white brick single storey building added at east end (behind the overhead mast in the 1997 photo).

The chimney at the west end of the house section was enlarged out c1890 to accommodate an extra fireplace in the new Booking Hall.
Hythe, Great Bentley, and Kirby Cross had/have white brick chimneys, whereas Alresford and Weeley have red brick chimneys.

bottom right
The complete bodily lifting of the existing station footbridges carried out in 1955 for the Southend line electrification was not repeated in subsequent electrification schemes. Instead, some footbridges got replacement higher spans, and entirely new footbridges were built at other stations.
The new 1957 footbridge at Frinton, seen here, represents a standard concrete type of 1957/8 which can also be seen at Ockendon, West Horndon, Pitsea, Weeley, and Thorpe-le-Soken. Different designs were used from 1959 on.

Platform canopy (1950s?, vice 1888 canopy) erected from second-hand materials including ex-LT&SR line brackets (see p.63).
Goods Lock-up 1903/4, hipped roof, narrower extension at west end for storeroom c1910.

Down platform, disused, 1937/8, with red brick rear wall and brick open shelter with concrete roof.
Footbridge, concrete, 1957.

Station Master's house 1910/11 (contract to H.Linzell 6.10.1910 at £412). Now doctors' surgery, extended and heavily altered.
Gate House, 1867 (see p.20). Now occupied by Frinton & Walton Heritage Trust and open to the public on Tuesday mornings.
Gate hut, 1880s?, see p.69. 15-lever ground frame.

Further Reading – GE Journal 110.

WALTON-ON-NAZE

Main buildings 1867, now converted to flats. The two storey end block remains in original form but has been roughcast since the 1960s at least. The single-storey east-west range on the north side had its west end demolished by a train in 1987 (since partly replaced by a new section c2001). The two storey 'tower' in this range had its upper half removed in the 1960s but this has been replaced c2001 by a smaller pastiche upper storey. The canopy brackets along the south side of the east-west range and the west side of the end block are original but the glass roofing carried on them is all new.

Single storey white brick hipped-roof Booking Office building 1989 (separate from the 1867 buildings).
Timber-built platform canopy/shelter, c1930.

Three weatherboarded cottages opposite station are believed to be those built c1880 and then purchased by GER 1883.

Further Reading – GE Journal 94.

In saying, for the purposes of overall analysis, that the ironwork at different stations is to the 'same' design, this does not necessarily mean absolutely identical, as different foundries would inevitably produce minor variations even when working from the same drawings. This is illustrated by the columns and capitals at Ingatestone up side, Newport (p.44), Wivenhoe, and Great Bentley up side. No two of these are identical in all respects.

The Newport columns are as Wivenhoe (p.44); the Ingatestone columns omit the Tudor roses; and the Great Bentley columns (far left photo here) omit the Tudor roses, and have two plain rings instead of the knobbed ring above the base section.

The capitals (actually part of the same casting as the columns) are almost identical at Newport and Wivenhoe. The Ingatestone capitals are the same except for the absence of the *volutes* below. But the Great Bentley capitals are significantly different and have no decoration below save for two circular protrusions on the plain column above the ring.

The brackets are virtually identical, but there is one little variation, which we will leave to the reader!

left A larger version of the same bracket design featured in the canopies put up at several of the Stour Valley line stations in the 1880s. The four columns (and brackets) from the Glemsford canopy were used by the CVR in the erection of their so-called 'Halstead' station building, as seen here. The columns are shorter than normal, because of the size of the brackets, and as they are also of above-average diameter they have a very stumpy appearance. The *volutes* below the capitals are of the Wivenhoe type.

all photos above
Details of the unique Thorpe-le-Soken 1866 station building, taken shortly after its recent renovation.

right
The 1882 island platform waiting rooms block at Thorpe-le-Soken. Compare Buckhurst Hill up side at p.43.

More details of Tendring Hundred Railway buildings.

left Road side windows at Great Bentley.

middle Window at rear of the St Botolph's 1866 building.

below The standard type wooden eaves level 'canopy' at Alresford.

11. ST BOTOLPH'S BRANCH

BRIDGE 1004, underbridge, River Colne, GR 008251. Two parallel girder spans (one for each track), 1925?, on brick abutments.

ST BOTOLPH'S / COLCHESTER TOWN

C18 house, purchased by THR and used as their office/board room, later Station Master's house.

Main building 1865/6, THR special design (see p.19). Canopy on front added by GER 1884 (photo p.43).

Station platform is built over cellars at west end and these are visible at rear. Platform canopy largely?/wholly? reconstructed 1991 as pastiche of original.

Further Reading – Railway Bylines Vol.10 No.3 (February 2005).

12. [WIVENHOE] TO BRIGHTLINGSEA

Current Status of Trackbed

Wivenhoe Jn (GR 042216) to GR 053208	Formation/embankment intact, no access
GR 053208 to GR 058199	Public or permitted footpath
GR 058199 to GR 059198 (north end of former swing bridge)	Embankment walkable

[There is no way across Alresford Creek – the ford at GR 063196 is not passable – the remainder of the route has to be walked from the Brightlingsea end].

GR 059196 (south end of former swing bridge) to GR 060195	Embankment walkable
GR 060195 to end of identifiable embankment at GR 076163	Embankment, public footpath
GR 076163 to terminus at GR 083166	Eliminated

BRIDGE 1035, ALRESFORD CREEK SWING BRIDGE. Demolished apart from two cylinders on each bank. (See p.144).

Corrugated iron clad boathouse for bridgeman (LNER) on north bank, derelict.

BRIGHTLINGSEA

[There are no remains of Brightlingsea station. For photo of the 1906 buildings see Paye].

Further Reading – P. Paye, The Brightlingsea Branch, John Masters, 1997.

13. [THORPE-LE-SOKEN] TO CLACTON

BRIDGE 1031, underbridge, Holland Brook, GR 193197. 1922?, widened 1936? No access.

BURRS ROAD LEVEL CROSSING. Crossing keeper's house, c1930 (photo p.53).

CLACTON

[For demolished 1882 station building see photo p.138].

Station buildings and concourse roofing 1929 (see p.70). Canopy on platforms 1/2 1929, reroofed and greatly reduced in length 1980s. [Canopy/shelters on platforms 3/4 demolished].

GER coach body, derelict (see GE Journal 100.66 for details).

Electric Traction Maintenance Depot 1981.
Terrace of six cottages 1885 (see p.50).

Signal Box 1891, GER Type 7 box, timber, rewindowed and reclad c2000. 52-lever Saxby & Farmer 1888 pattern Duplex frame, 1891.

[1928 Loco Shed, at GR 179160, is now demolished except for the short corrugated asbestos extension section of 1958].

Further Reading – British Railways Illustrated Vol.9 No.4 (1930s photosurvey).

14. FRINTON TO WALTON OLD LINE

Current Status of Trackbed

GR 238204 to GR 241205	Formation eliminated
GR 241205 to GR 246206	Roads (Waltham Way and The Leas) are directly on trackbed
GR 246206 to GR 248209	No trace of formation, The Greensward covers site. In the middle portion of this section the line was just beyond the present cliff top.
GR 248209 to GR 249213	Formation eliminated (however, the rear garden fences of the houses on the west side of Woodberry Way are on the alignment of the railway's up side fence).

15. [MANNINGTREE] TO HARWICH

BRIDGE 1043, underbridge, Station Road, GR 100321. 1854, red brick, 30ft span arch, skew.

BRIDGE 1046, overbridge, South Street, GR 106316. 1854, 30ft span three-centred arch, skew. Originally red brick but mostly refaced in engineering brick.

BRIDGE 1047, overbridge, Oxford Road, GR 108316. 1854, 30ft span three-centred arch. Mostly red brick, white brick arch.

MISTLEY

Station building/house 1854, red brick with gault brick dressings, see p.16. Single storey extension at west end c1880. Single storey sections at east end part original?

Some track remains on Mistley Quay (GR 117319).

Further Reading – GE Journal 97.

BRADFIELD

[No remains of station buildings or platforms. For photos of demolished building see p.138].

BRIDGE 1056, underbridge, Shore Lane, GR 144313. 1854, red brick with white brick for arch and imposts, 20ft span segmental arch, skew. Photo p.17.

BRIDGE 1057, underbridge, occupation, GR 151313. 1854, red brick, 12ft span semicircular arch. Photo p.3.

BRIDGE 1059, underbridge, Wheatsheaf Lane, GR 168314. 1854, red brick originally but much strengthened and refaced in engineering brick, 19ft9in span semicircular arch.

WRABNESS

[1854 station building demolished. For photo see p.17].

One pair of cottages in Church Road (GR 177316). 1886, Shenfield type (see p.51). Contract to W.T.Hook 7.9.1886 at £430. Badly altered.

Further Reading – GE Journal 104.

BRIDGE 1063, underbridge, occupation, GR 187316. 1854, red brick, 12ft span semicircular-arch 'tunnel'.

PARKESTON QUAY / HARWICH INTERNATIONAL

Parkeston Quay Hotel (alias Great Eastern Hotel) / station offices building (now port offices) 1883, see p.54.

Station entrance block on up side (red brick, flat roof), footbridge, and platform canopies all 1972.

Bridge 1043, east side.

above left Although it is not in the GER-built section of Parkeston village, it seems appropriate to include a view of the entrance to the 'Hamilton Hall' at the rear of the Garland Hotel (now the 'Captain Fryatt').

above right The 1866 Harwich station had (despite its proximity to the crowded town centre) been built on open ground, and was provided with a large forecourt approach. In January 1882 the GER Board approved a plan to install tasteful shrubberies plus this drinking fountain. The local press reported this work complete in December.

The 1882 Dovercourt platform canopy features longitudinal girders (and, in consequence, four brackets per column), although it was erected six years before longitudinal girders became a standard feature of GER canopies.

below

The memorial erected by the GER company to Capt. Fryatt in 1920 stands on the north side of Dovercourt churchyard at the end of a specially made pathway down from the church. It was planned to have a view over the river as background but the insensitively planned postwar housing immediately behind spoilt that.

Fryatt was Captain of the GER Harwich – Hook of Holland steamer S.S. *Brussels*, which was captured by German naval vessels on 23rd June 1916. He was put on trial at Bruges on 27th July for an incident in 1915 when the *Brussels* had tried to ram a German U-boat, found guilty of being a *franc-tireur*, and executed the same evening. The Germans had been annoyed at the way in which the GER had been successfully continuing the Hook service during the war. The incident brought outrage in the British and overseas press, comparable with that after the previous case of Edith Cavell. Fryatt was buried in Bruges but after the war his body was exhumed and, after what was virtually a state funeral at St Paul's Cathedral, was reinterred here at Dovercourt in July 1919. The memorial was unveiled on 18th June 1920 by Lord Claud Hamilton who was High Steward of the Borough of Harwich in addition to being Chairman of the GER. It had been made by Messrs Farmer & Hindley of Westminster Bridge Road, in Portland stone.

Another memorial to Fryatt had been erected in the main (west side) Booking Hall at Liverpool Street in 1917, presented to the GER by the Netherlands section of the League of Neutral States. This is now to be found on the re-erected War Memorial at the rebuilt station.

The *Brussels* was later sunk at Zeebrugge, but was raised after the war and returned to active service, but not with the GER/LNER.

left

There are of course many other GER maritime staff buried at Dovercourt. The most notable group of memorials are those to some of the victims of the loss of the GER's S.S. *Berlin* in a storm off Hook of Holland on 21st February 1907. This is the grandiose memorial to Chief Steward William Moor, 'subscribed for by personal friends'. His Captain John Precious lies more modestly beside him. (The *Berlin* memorials were erected privately, not by the GER).

Parkeston Quay Passenger Terminal building (to west of Hotel block) 1972.

Signal Box 1987, red brick.

[The Quay itself was built 1879-83 with western extensions 1905-7 and 1931-4. All pre-1960s buildings on the quays are now demolished].

PARKESTON VILLAGE

74 GER cottages, being

One pair in Makins Road, non-GER design, 1884. See p.56.

Two terraces of six cottages each at north end of Hamilton Street, probably c1885. See p.56.

Two terraces of ten cottages each at north end of Tyler Street, 1890. See p.56.

Two terraces of ten cottages each on south side of Foster Road, 1899/1900. See p.56.

Two terraces of ten cottages each on north side of Foster Road, 1913 or soon after. See p.57.

Enginemen's Barracks, 1899/1900, now 'Hamilton House', see p.57.

CAPT. FRYATT'S MEMORIAL, DOVERCOURT CHURCHYARD. Erected by GER 1920.

DOVERCOURT

Station building/house 1854, red brick with gault brick dressings, see p.17. One of the original small blocks on the platform side remains; with that exception the 1854 covered area was removed 1882/3 when the present canopy (see p.42) was added. Canopy is of full original length and width.

Gabled red brick block to east of main building, c1900?

Open Gents to east of last, date not known.

To west of passenger entrance, brick base for Water Tank 1863.

[Down platform and buildings demolished].

Further Reading – GE Journal 129.

HARWICH TOWN

(See pp.26-28 for more information and photographs).

[For 1854 station building see p.136].

Main station building 1865/6, single storey, white brick. See p.25. Lower section at south end c1880s. [Station Master's house section at north end demolished].

Platform canopy, c1985 reconstruction of two bays only of original canopy, new columns, GER 1860s style valancing.

[Island platform, and structures, demolished].

GER boundary wall along west side of George St, 1865/6, white brick.

GER drinking fountain in station forecourt, 1882. Made by George Smith & Co, Sun Foundry, Glasgow.

Stables, 1913 (see p.67).

Goods Shed with office, yellow brick, 1865, derelict. East side considerably altered and canopy removed.

Great Eastern Hotel, 1865 (now 'Quayside Court'). Boundary wall to East Gate Street, 1865?, red brick.

Halfpenny Pier alias Corporation Pier, built 1852/3 for Harwich Corporation, was railway-owned 1872-1974. [Outer end of main pier removed, east arm altered].

Halfpenny Pier Booking Office and Waiting Room, built by GER c1890s. Photos p.2 and p.28.

Continental Pier alias Trinity House Pier, built by GER 1865/6, outer end rebuilt in concrete 1915-21, pier reduced in width 1957. Now owned by Trinity House.

Train Ferry Pier 1924. Link span was second hand from Southampton (1917 there), gantry was second hand from Richborough (1917 there). Derelict.

Further Reading – GERS Journal Special No.2 (Parkeston and Harwich); GE Journal 93; British Railways Illustrated Vol.2 No.6 (Train Ferry).

The Train Ferry gantry as viewed from one of the ships in the early years of the service. The towers housed counterweights for the hoisting machinery which was located in the operator's cabin. The 120ft linkspan used at Harwich was the longest of the five built for the War Department in 1917. Shunting could be done on a gradient of up to 1 in 20, up to the ship at high tide or down at low tide. The gantry is in a virtually unchanged state today.

The Corporation *alias* Halfpenny Pier c1890, with the GER cargo ship *Harwich* alongside the main section of the pier. Part of the eastern arm of the pier is seen at right. In the foreground are the second Booking Office and Waiting Room, which did not last long after this.

GER/LNER Shotley Ferry Boats - the following survive:

- *Pin Mill* (built 1910, bought by GER 1912) currently at Faversham Iron Wharf under restoration
- *Hainault* (1914) last reported abandoned at Pin Mill
- *Brightlingsea* (1924) recently completed restoration at Woodbridge.

This view shows better the linkspan, here sloped up to the ship at high tide, and the Train Ferry 'Pier', which was actually a 'dock' into which the ships reversed.

16. MANNINGTREE NORTH CURVE

BRIDGE 1042, underbridge, GR 099322. 1882, red brick, semicircular arch (now rendered).

17. MISTLEY THORPE & WALTON RAILWAY

The earthworks for this line were constructed in 1864-8 from the junction east of Mistley (GR 127318) to Thorpe Road, Tendring (GR 153241). The then-surviving cuttings were deepened in 1940 to serve as a Tank Trap but much was then filled in again after the war.

The current OS 1/25000 map does show most of the surviving earthworks and should be compared with the 1875 6in maps here (p.116) which show the whole of the constructed line. Blank sections on these maps simply indicate that the line was level with the surrounding fields at those points.

The principal works extant are:

A Harwich Road overbridge (GR 131314). Segmental arch, skew. Now filled in and the parapet walls as seen from the road are the only visible trace. (The formation of the line is also marked by a field boundary to the north of this bridge).

B – C Cutting (altered 1940). Accessible from Essex Way footpath.

D – E Formation marked by long line of trees. Not accessible but can be seen from footpath to the east.

F Embankment on south side of present Tendring Road, built to carry the road over the line. (Formation also marked by hedge line for 300yds south from here).

G Brick walling on north side of road believed to be the remains of MT&WR bridge.

H Remains of railway embankment on private land between road and fields.

['Arch Cottages' on the north side of the A120 at GR 133277 (shown as 'Brickkiln House' on 1875 map) are named after the MT&WR railway bridge that was built here but there are now no remains of this bridge].

Further Reading – T.B.Peacock, The Mistley Thorpe & Walton Railway, 1946.

Looking east along Tendring Road (GR 139267). The trees and bushes on the south side of the road are growing on the embankment built to carry the road up to an intended bridge over the line.

View south from GR 150247 towards Tendring Grove Wood. The formation line is still shown as a track on current OS maps but is actually in the last stages of decay.

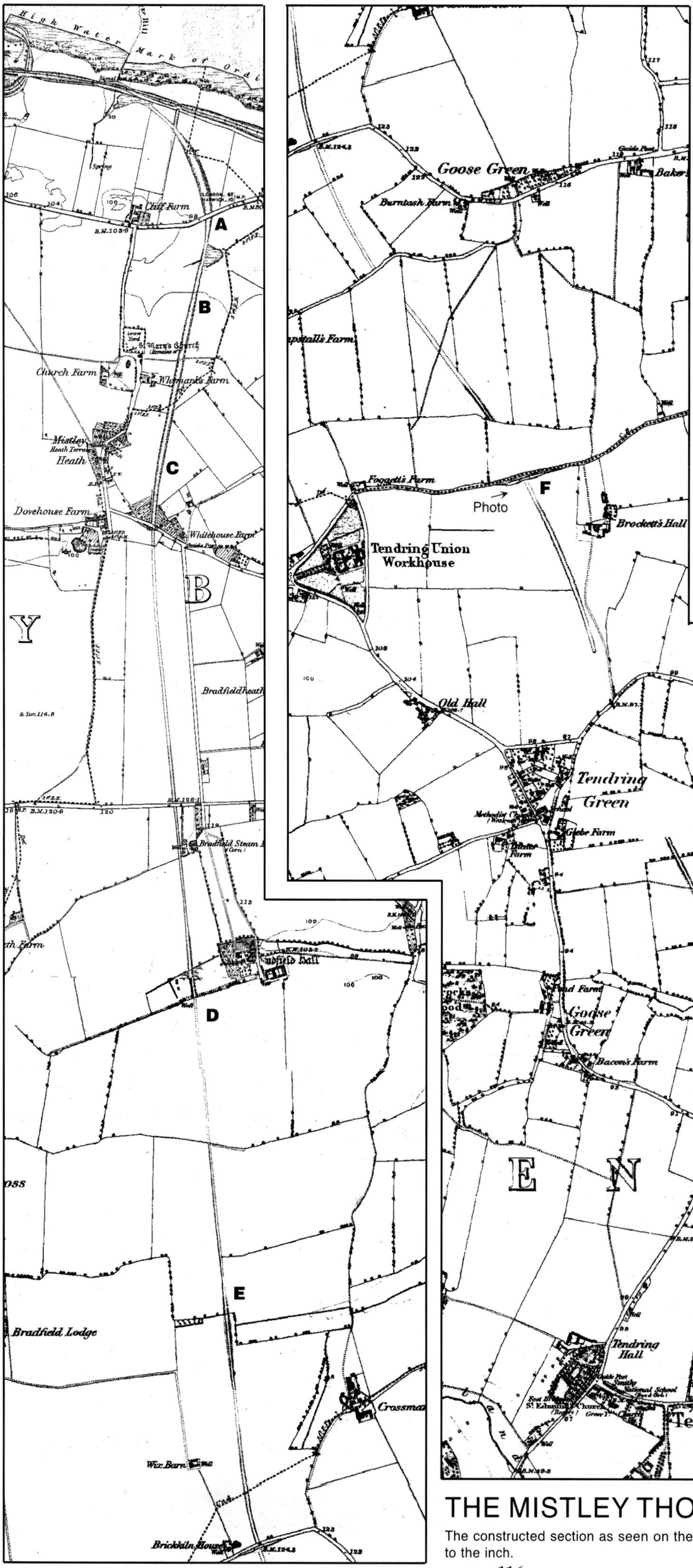

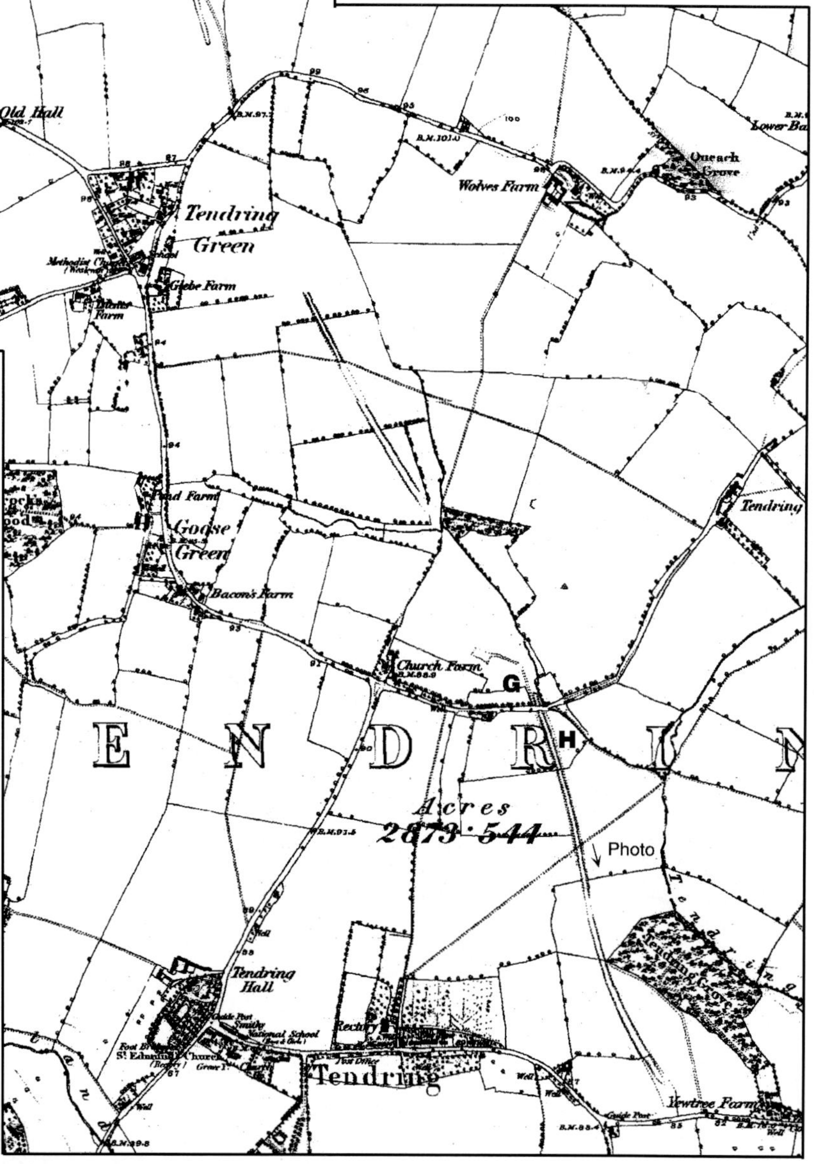

THE MISTLEY THORPE & WALTON RAILWAY

The constructed section as seen on the 1st edition OS 6in map, reduced to a scale of 4 miles to the inch.

18. PARKESTON ABANDONED LINE

Current Status of Trackbed

Junction at GR221317 to Ray Lane (GR223317) — Intact, overgrown, fenced off.
Ray Lane to new A120 at GR238317 — Stretches remain across golf course, no access.
New A120 to Parkeston Road (GR240317) — Intact, overgrown, accessible.
For 40yds east from Parkeston Road — Private garden.
GR241317 to GR246318 — Cutting intact, tarmac footpath.
GR246318 to junction at GR248318 — Overgrown.

BRIDGE 1073, overbridge, Parkeston Road, GR240317. c1880, red brick, two iron girder spans with central brick pillar.

BRIDGE 1074, Parkeston Road bridge over Ramsey Creek stream, GR239318. (Parkeston Road was built by the GER). c1880, red brick, three segmental arches.

GATE HOUSE at former level crossing GR241317. 1854? Single storey, much altered and extended. (This LC was closed after Parkeston Road was built).

above Bridge 1073 from the west. The old line was lifted shortly after the new loop via Parkeston Quay opened (although it is not clear that this had originally been intended). This bridge and 1074 both have double-bullnose coping bricks made by the same firm as those on the '1865' lines (p.123), although the wording here is 'JOSEPH HAMBLET WEST BROMWICH STAFFORDSHIRE' and there is also an anchor symbol.

right Bridge 1074 was one of the most substantial of the GER's three dozen 'side bridges', i.e. bridges that were not over or under a railway line. (Most such bridges carried public roads over streams at places where the road had been rebuilt by the railway when the line was built, on the approach to a bridge over the railway).

Parkeston Road was built by the GER as there was no existing convenient access road between the main road through Dovercourt and the Parkeston Quay area. At this point it slopes down from south to north, and all the brickwork above the arching in this bridge is parallel with the top of the parapet wall, not in horizontal courses.

below The original Harwich branch line south of Parkeston-to-be, as seen on the 1875 OS 6in map, reduced to a scale of four inches to the mile. The positions of the junctions with the 1882/3 loop line are marked X - X. The abandoned section of the line had two level crossings, at Ray Lane at the west end of this extract, and at the unnamed lane leading to Dovercourt Dock. Both had gatehouses; there are no known photographs of the Ray Lane gatehouse which is long demolished, but the Dovercourt Dock gatehouse is still standing, although the lane it served was taken out of use after Parkeston Road was opened. The abandoned section of the line was on low embankment for much of its length, but in cutting west of Ray Lane, and from just west of Parkeston Road to 450 yds east of the Gatehouse.

Ramsey Ray Island had already lost some of its insularity with the reclamation of the former large areas of salt marsh either side of Ramsey Creek when the embankment was built between Dovercourt Dock and Delf Pond. (This embankment was later incorporated into the GER's wider Parkeston Road embankment). The saltings north of Dovercourt Dock were then reclaimed in 1879-83 in connection with the construction of the new loop line, and much of 'Ray Creek' and 'Sunk Island' also disappeared under GER fill.

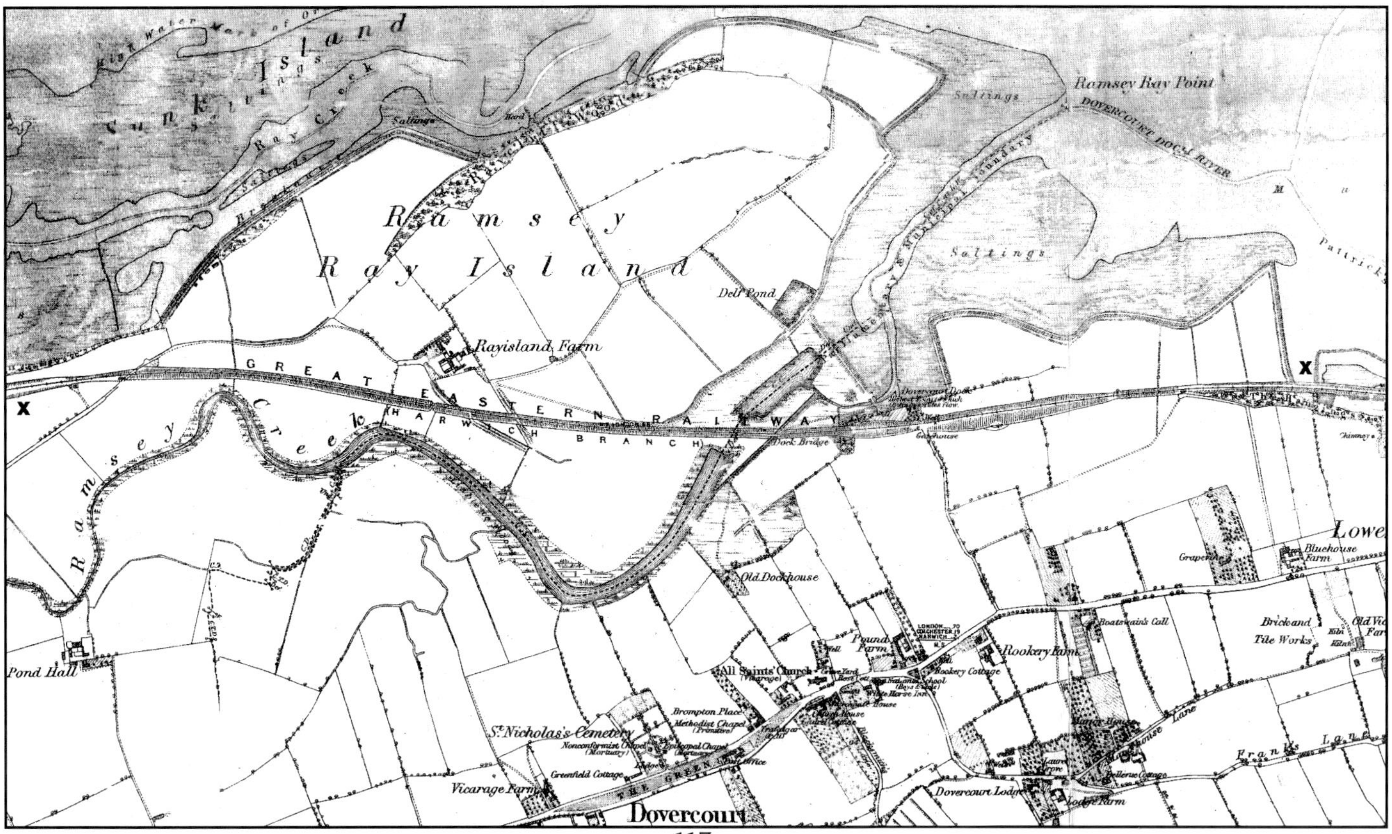

19. CAMBRIDGE MAIN LINE, ROYDON TO GREAT CHESTERFORD

ROYDON

Station building/house N&ER 1841, see p.9. Now a restaurant. Platform canopy behind largely dates from c1990 'restoration' and is shorter, narrower, and lower than its predecessor. Like its predecessor it has MkI 'standard' valancing.

Small Booking Office building on up platform, 1970s?

Signal Box 1876, GER Type 1 box but unrecognisable as extended at both ends and to front in C20. Boarded up.

Goods Shed, brick, 1840s, derelict.

Two cottages (191/193 High Street) on west side of road north of LC, 1864.

Further Reading - GE Journal 101.

BRIDGE 1444, underbridge, Stort Navigation, GR 408105. Recent steel girder span.

HARLOW TOWN

New station 1960. Plaque in Booking Hall commemorates formal opening on 13.7.1960. All still largely in original condition. High Booking Hall and lower office wings. Wide footbridge with three lift towers. Waiting Rooms are on footbridge. Interior walls in blue mosaic. No platform buildings and only short canopies with steel columns and timber ceilings.

HARLOW MILL

Main building/house N&ER 1841, see p.10. Everything to the east of the entrance porch now demolished, also the shaped gables have been removed from the remaining section of the building.

Gents, c1880s, brown brick, at west end of main building, derelict.

Footbridge, concrete,1960.

Signal Box, BR(ER) Type 18 box, 1960, disused.

SAWBRIDGEWORTH

(The present station is wholly north of the level crossing in Hertfordshire, but the original main building was south of the LC in Essex).

Main Booking Office building on down side, white brick with flat roof, date not known (1960s?). Waiting Rooms block on up platform in same style.

Footbridge, concrete, 1959.

BRIDGE 1473, underbridge, Stort Navigation, GR 490158. Reconstructed 1931, 30ft steel girder span with longitudinal trough girders over river (skew), 13ft span over flood opening.

BRIDGE 1479, underbridge, Stort Navigation, GR 493202. Reconstructed 1931, 53ft5in steel girder span over river, 28ft6in span for flood opening.

BISHOPS STORTFORD

(This station is and always was in Hertfordshire).

Main building 1845 (new station authorised by ECR Board 30.9.1845). Three-storey block in the same vein and the same buff brick as Audley End and Great Chesterford. Originally had stuccoed quoins, a stuccoed string course below the second floor windows, and a heavily dentillated cornice (see photo at Paye p.85); but all these details are now gone. Also spoilt by recent replacement windows. There may have originally been full flat canopies as at Audley End / Great Chesterford; part of that on the road side remains (older maps not helpful).

Booking Hall/Office 1960/1, all glass walling.

Down platform canopy early 1880s (post 1879 OS), see photo p.42. A short section adjacent to the new Booking Hall was removed 1960/1 and new canopy erected in lieu here. Valancing removed 1960/1.

(Immediately north of Booking Hall). Base of former water tank (1867), yellow brick, three semicircular-arched windows with 'keystones'. Tank removed, new upper floor added for conversion to offices 1960/1.

(Immediately north of the last). Round base of former water tank (c1870). Tank removed and base converted to offices 1960/1, brickwork wholly refaced.

Footbridge 1959, altered after 1990 fire.

Up side Booking Office 1899 (contract to J.Glass 7.2.1899 at £960). Red brick, hipped roof, canopy on front and on both sides (photo p.47). Original 'Booking Hall' glass in rear windows.

Up platform building c1960/1. For up platform canopy see p.119.

Bishops Stortford South Signal Box, 1931, LNER Type 11b box, brick to floor construction, jettied, disused and boarded up.

top left
The Roydon staff cottages, which very much exemplify the pokiness of much earlier staff housing that the GER tried to improve on in the 1880s and '90s. The contract for these cottages was given to Perry & Judson on 13th October 1864 at only £150 each.

top right
Detail of the timber columns at Roydon, also showing the uniquely-styled valancing added at an unknown date in the late GER / early LNER period.

bottom
Roydon goods shed, the earliest surviving goods shed in Essex, built prior to 1847. An identical goods shed formerly existed at Ponders End (see GE Journal 116.38).

left

The 1845 Bishops Stortford building viewed from the up platform in 1982, when it did at least retain the old window sashes. The 'ghosts' of the stucco quoins and string course are evident due to the brickwork having retained its original colour whilst the rest had become smoke-darkened. (The brickwork has all been cleaned subsequently, making the building look quite 'dead'). Note the large semicircular-arched ground floor openings; the window-door-window arrangement here on the platform side is as at Audley End.

below left

This original window survives in the single storey block at the south end of the 1845 building, road side. It is to the same design as the ground floor windows at Audley End. The arrangement of the walling here also reminds one of the Audley End porte-cochere.

below centre

The awning on the road side of the Bishops Stortford 1845 building looks all modern at first glance but in fact there is just a new fascia hiding the old work which is similar to Audley End. The bracket may be a later addition for strengthening as at Audley End.

below right

Somewhat oddly, the 3rd 4th and 5th columns (from the south end) of the Bishops Stortford down platform canopy have columns and brackets which, whilst clearly intended to be the same as the others, must come from a different casting. They have 'flat' features whereas the others (p.42) are rounded off.

below left and right

The Bishops Stortford up platform canopy is an interesting puzzle! The platform itself dates from 1869 and originally had no canopy. A minute of 4.11.1874 authorised the erection of a canopy but the date at which the work was actually done is not known. The canopy as existing in the late C19 was the same length as the present canopy.

On 10.5.1926, during the General Strike, the greater part of it was demolished in a train collision, killing one passenger in the process. The 1.35pm Cambridge to Liverpool Street, standing at the Up Main platform, was run into by an up goods train which had left Cambridge under time interval working and had gradually caught up with it. The driver of the express was an experienced locoman, having been a fireman on the Midland for some years prior to the war, but had never been on this line before. The time interval working was also not being handled very well. By a strange coincidence, the only other serious accidents during the Strike both occurred on this same day - the well-known derailing of a passenger train at Cramlington, and a collission between a passenger train and a line of wagons at St Margaret's (Edinburgh) which caused three fatalities.

In December 1926 the LNER minutes record that, to replace ten bays of this canopy (shown on an accompanying plan as being the first ten bays from the footbridge), 'an awning which had been removed from Newmarket Old High Level Station' was to be re-erected at Bishops Stortford, and that the materials had already been delivered to the site. Alfred Coe of Bishops Stortford was given the job of re-erecting it, as the Engineer had no staff of his own available. (This must be taken as referring to the 1885 High Level island platform at Newmarket Old (?) which was outside the trainshed roof. The canopy on this platform was 24ft wide, 333ft long, and of the same width throughout, whereas the up platform canopy at Bishops Stortford is 229ft long and of varying width; so even as originally intended it was not simply a case of re-erecting a complete canopy as it stood).

Examination of the present up platform canopy shows that it actually combines elements from three different sources, and that it was erected to a quite different arrangement to that shown in the contract plan, with fewer columns, more widely spaced.

The first pair of columns at the north (footbridge) end, and their brackets – photo below left – are of the Mildenhall branch type. They might have come from one of those stations as several of the canopies on the branch were reduced in length at this time.

There are then three single columns, followed by four pairs of columns – photo below right – of a design not known elsewhere but clearly of 1870s/80s date. Did these columns come from Newmarket?? The brackets on these columns are however of the same type as found on the majority of the down platform canopy. It is possible that these brackets may be salvaged from the previous wrecked canopy, as it is unlikely that all the brackets would have been broken beyond reuse. Alternatively, the Newmarket Old canopy, no good photographs of which are known, may also have had brackets of this type.

Finally there are two pairs of columns at the south end, one pair at each end of the platform building, with both columns and brackets of the same type as those in the down platform canopy. Given what is shown in the contract plan, plus the fact that the pre-1926 platform buildings lasted into the 1950s (see photo Paye p.86), it seems clear that this southern end of the original canopy survived the collision.

It can therefore be concluded that the whole of the pre-1926 up platform canopy was to the same design as the down platform canopy, in which case it too must have dated from 1880-82.

The rear of the Stansted station house, with the extension at left. The bay window on the 1845 section is probably not original. In this 1982 photograph the overall dirt of decades rather obscures the fact that both the original section and the extension are in bright red brick with white brick dressings. The brickwork has since been cleaned.

The down platform Waiting Room at Elsenham, with the Gents beyond (photo 1982).

This pair of cottages for the signalmen at the new intermediate signal box at North Hall were authorised in August 1874 at an estimate of £400 – a low figure considering their size. In May 1875 Swarbrick the GER General Manager visited these cottages and it was resolved that this design should become standard. However this did not happen.

Newport Viaduct – the 5th 4th and 3rd arches as seen from the down side.

BRIDGE 1489, overbridge, Stansted Road, GR 505240. Lengthy side walling (1845?) with blank arcading, very skew bridge. (Recent concrete span).

STANSTED MOUNTFITCHET

Station house 1845, red brick with white brick dressings (see p.10). Single-storey lean-to section on south side may be original given that Newport is the same. Building extended (1850s?) with two-storey north-south gabled wing and flat-roof section at north end.

1850s? ECR type small canopy on large brackets on platform side of house.

Remainder of down platform canopy, and rear brick wall, plus canopy over passenger entrance on road side of wall, 1889/90. (Improvements at Stansted authorised August 1889 at estimate of £1,266).

Up platform canopy (photo p.41) and rear brick wall, also timber Waiting Rooms block on up platform, 1889/90.

(The canopies have 'standard' columns with transverse brackets only. They had MkII standard valancing; this was replaced by plain valancing by the 1960s, then in the 1980s both canopies were reduced in width for electrification and new straight sawtooth valancing provided).

Footbridge, concrete staircases and steel span, c1986.

ELSENHAM

Station house 1845, red brick with brighter red brick dressings; original single-storey gable-to-track section on east side (see p.10). House extended on west side in yellow brick, with lean-to roof, date not known.

Flat-roof red brick Waiting Room on down platform, c1938 (after previous buildings destroyed by fire). To the north of this flat-roof red brick Gents, date not known.

Up side Booking Office building, red brick, gabled, 1913? (see p.41).

Up platform timber-built Waiting Rooms block plus canopy, 1902 (see p.41). 'Standard' columns, transverse brackets only, MkII standard valancing. Canopy cut back in width for electrification c1985, original valancing reused.

Crossing keeper's hut, large gabled timber building, late C20.

Two GER platform seats (on up platform).

NORTH HALL. Pair of cottages for signalmen, 1875. (Nos 1 and 2 Railway Cottages, on east side of North Hall Road, west of line, GR 524302).

NEWPORT

Station house 1845, red brick with white brick dressings. Single-storey lean-to section (as Stansted) on west side.

Remainder of station buildings and platform canopies 1884/5, see p.25 and p.44 for details. Canopies cut back in width for electrification c1985. The valancing on the front of the up platform canopy is new-made 1980s.

'GER' fireplaces in Booking Hall (same design as that in Chappel B.O., p.38 photo), up side Waiting Room (same design as that in Chappel Goods Shed office, p.106 photo), and possibly others.

Porters' Room (on down platform south of footbridge), date not known, served as 'signal box' 1972-1983.

Footbridge c1986, plate steel span.

Further Reading – GE Journal 98.

BRIDGE 1514, NEWPORT VIADUCT, GR 522345. 1845, low viaduct of thirteen segmental arches, much altered, and impossible to appreciate as a whole owing to the crowded surroundings. The 4th arch from the south end is over the Debden Water stream; the 5th over Water Lane (road); the 8th over Bridge End (road); and the 13th over an occupation track. Older portions of the viaduct are in a reddish-yellow brick. Most arches have a 4-course understrengthening in engineering brick.

BRIDGE 1516, AUDLEY END VIADUCT, GR 516361. 1845, seven arches of 20ft span, 60ft high at centre. Photo back cover.

AUDLEY END

Main building/House 1845, see p.11. Porte-cochere assumed 1845. Late C20 single storey extension to building at north end in original style for shop.

Flat canopy on platform side has two 'GER' type brackets added for extra support.

Large waiting shelter building at south end of up platform, 1980s.

Footbridge c1980, concrete stairs and steel span.

Down platform Waiting Rooms block and canopy 1894 (contract 3.7.1894 to Collins & Barber at £360). Canopy has 'standard' columns, with quarter-circle longitudinal brackets, see p.46.

Small Waiting Area / Station Master's Office block on Saffron Walden branch platform, yellow brick, gabled, date not known.

Further Reading – GE Journal 100.

AUDLEY END TUNNEL. 1845, decorative south portal (p.12), plain north portal.

LITTLEBURY TUNNEL. 1845, Egyptian south portal, plain north portal.

GREAT CHESTERFORD

Main building/House 1845, see p.11.

Booking Office building 1980s?

Footbridge, concrete stairs and steel span, c1986.

Further Reading – GE Journal 92.

ICKLETON ROAD. Gate House, 1845, see p.53.

20. [BISHOPS STORTFORD] TO [BRAINTREE]

Current Status of Trackbed

Bishops Stortford to Bridge 2071 at GR 516212	No significant remains
Bridge 2071 to GR 613216 (Dunmow)	Owned by ECC, 'Flitch Way' path/cycleway (except route is now cut by new A120 at GR 607214, only a few yards of the trackbed are lost but longer diversions are in place for walkers)
GR 613216 to GR 635213 (Dunmow)	Road on formation
GR 635213 to east end of former viaduct at GR 637211	Eliminated
GR 637211 to west end of Braintree station (GR 760227)	Owned by ECC, 'Flitch Way' path/cycleway

All remaining bridges on this line are listed here (except for small unnumbered culverts).

BRIDGE 2069, overbridge, Dunmow Road (Nags Head), GR 502213. 1865, white brick, 25ft span three-centred arch. Not accessible at formation level, little visible at road level.

BRIDGE 2071, underbridge, occupation and stream, GR 516212. Date not known, girder span, brick abutments. Poor condition, overgrown.

BRIDGE 2072, underbridge, Hallingbury Road, GR 519212. 1894?? reconstruction, 23ft10in span girders and corrugated cross troughing, plate sided, red brick abutments with later strengthening in engineering brick.

BRIDGE 2073, underbridge, Stane Street Halt, GR 548212. 1894 reconstruction, 24ft9in span girders and corrugated cross troughing, plate sided, red brick abutments. Photo p.124.

BRIDGE 2074, overbridge, (Takeley) Station Road, GR 561211. 1865, white brick, 25ft2in span three-centred arch, slightly skew. Photo p.122.

TAKELEY

Station building/house '1865' 'small' type, 1865/6, all white brick. Gents (1865?) at east end. Long derelict but restored 2006 by ECC, now Ranger's office for Flitch Way. Photo p.94.

Goods Lock-up, yellow brick, gabled, 1881. (Approved by Board 20.10.1880).

Station platform.

Further Reading - GE Journal 122; P. Paye, The Bishops Stortford Dunmow & Braintree Branch.

BRIDGE 2075, overbridge, Canfield Road, GR 568211. 1865, white brick, 25ft 2in span three-centred arch, skew. Much patched in engineering brick. Photo p.122.

BRIDGE 2076, underbridge, occupation, GR 586212. 1865, red brick, 12ft1in span semicircular arch. Photo p.124.

BRIDGE 2077, underbridge, Church Lane, GR 587212. 1894 reconstruction, 24ft8in span girders and corrugated cross troughing, plate sided, red brick abutments.

EASTON LODGE

(GR 603213).

Crossing House (High Cross Lane) 1865/6, white brick, see p.24.

Crossing Keeper's hut, timber, lean-to roof, c1920?, see p.24.

Further Reading – P. Paye, The Bishops Stortford Dunmow & Braintree Branch.

BRIDGE 2079, overbridge, 'Folly Bridge', occupation, GR 617216. 1865, red brick, three segmental arches, centre arch 25ft1in, side arches 20ft3in. Photo p.124.

DUNMOW

[No remains: for demolished station buildings see p.95].

BRIDGE 2084, underbridge, 'Langleys', occupation, GR 638209. 1894?? reconstruction, 11ft5in girder span with longitudinal corrugated troughing, plate sided, red brick abutments.

BRIDGE 2085, underbridge, Clobbs Lane, GR 645208. 1895 reconstruction, 21ft10in span girders and corrugated cross troughing, plate sided, engineering brick abutments.

BISHOPS STORTFORD - BRAINTREE LINE SINGLE ARCH OVERBRIDGES

Bridge 2095 was illustrated at p.24 to show the standard design of three-centred-arch single-arch overbridge used on this line (and on the other 1865 lines, although there are none on the Ongar line). The bridges of this type still extant on this line are 2069, 2074, 2075, 2087, 2091, 2092, 2094, and 2095. 2080 has been demolished and 2078 has been filled in.

In span all are 25ft (plus or minus 3 inches).

In width most are 24ft to 26ft, but those carrying main roads (2069 and 2080) were 35ft wide, and 2091 carrying an occupation road is only 12ft6in wide.

In height (rail level to road surface level) those on this line vary only between 18ft and 20ft.

As with the station buildings, there are, once one starts looking, significant differences in the constructional details, of the upper portions in particular. In some cases this is clearly site-related, some roads having as big a 'hump' as the Highway Authority allowed the railway to get away with, others having a near-level road surface. However many of the differences are not so readily explicable. Again one is left to wonder how much was left to the contractor's men! (Some differences may however be due to later reconstruction/repair).

The string courses above the arch vary from three (2092, 2095) to six (2074) courses in width; the bottom course is always (2080 excepted) less proud than the others, the top course is always of chamfered bricks. Most bridges (*not* 2074, 2087) have a further chamfered course some 3-8 courses above the string course, which serves to reduce the width of the upper part of the parapet wall.

The string course is normally parallel to the parapet wall coping (as are all the courses in between). The amount of 'camber' in the coping normally reflects the gradients of the road surface. In cases where the parapet wall coping and the string course are almost horizontal (2080, 2095), the brickwork in the 'spandrels' (i.e. below the string course) may also be in parallel with them. But where the string course is significantly curved, the brickwork below is normally laid nearer to the horizontal, with a special gradually-rising-towards-the-middle course just below the string course.

[The various *other* types of bridge on this line are fully described on p.124.]

The bridges are in white brick from Bishops Stortford as far as 2075, and red brick from 2076 to Braintree. All are in English bond.

top left

Bridge 2074 at Takeley has a 'humped' roadway and the upper brickwork is significantly curved. The six-course string course here, with two chamfered courses at the top, is a little over-heavy. This string course is also odd in being some 8in clear of the head of the arch; in all the other bridges the head of the arch either meets or virtually meets the string course.

second left

Bridge 2075 has an almost-horizontal coping but, for reasons not evident, the string course (here of five courses width) is more curved. The 'adjustment' is made in the courses between the string course and the chamfered course above. The brickwork in the spandrels is in line with the string course. This bridge is slightly skewed (26ft8in span on the skew) but not enough to show in the arch rings. The arch has become deformed.

third left

The now-demolished Bridge 2080 at Dunmow. This was 24ft11in span at 90 degrees and 29ft0in on the skew. This level of skew is enough to show prominently in the arch rings. The arch is rather imperfectly made at bottom left. A unique feature here is that the bottom course of the string course was as proud as the others.

bottom left

Bridge 2087 has a four-course string course, and the parapet wall is of the same width throughout, i.e. there is no chamfered course higher up.

below

The narrow Bridge 2091 has been completely rebuilt in its upper parts, in plain reddish-grey brickwork with no string course. The yellowish bricks used in the original work are themselves unique on this line.

top left
Bridge 2092 is very similar to 2095, however the parapet wall and string course drop away more at either end, and a gradually-rising additional course is inserted below the string course to adjust.

top right
Bridge 2094 is on virtually the same degree of skew as 2080 (25ft1in span at 90 degrees, 28ft11in on the skew). The parapet coping and the four-course string course are all but horizontal, however the brickwork in the spandrels is not horizontal as one might expect but rises toward the centre!

far right
Detail of the arching at Bridge 2094. Here and at 2080 there is a sixth outer arch ring of bricks laid face on.

middle upper
A close view of the 'Hamblet Oldbury near Birmingham' markings on the double-bullnose coping bricks at Bridge 2092. All the bridges on the line have these coping bricks, and no doubt all were made by Hamblet's, however the great majority of them have no markings (indeed some bridges have no marked examples at all). Some (only a small percentage) of the marked bricks also have the '1865' date stamp as here. This stamping has the air of being done by a bored apprentice as one brick is date stamped thirteen times! Most Ongar line bridges also have these marked bricks.

middle lower
Bridge 2087 has coping bricks with a different wording 'Joseph Hamblet West Bromwich' (*cf* Bridges 1073 and 1074, p.117).

BRIDGE 2086, underbridge, 'Grangers', occupation, GR 656210. 1865, red brick, 8ft span semicircular arch, substantial wing walling.

BRIDGE 2087, overbridge, Brook Street (Little Dunmow), GR 658210. 1865, red brick, 25ft1in span three-centred arch (p.122).

FELSTED

Station building/house '1865' 'small' type, 1865/6, red brick with white brick dressings. Later lean-to extension against east wall of house. Gents (1865?) at west end. Photo p.94.
Goods Lock-up, gabled, date not known, derelict.
Scullery (in garden) 1865/6.

Further Reading - P. Paye, The Bishops Stortford Dunmow & Braintree Branch.

BRIDGE 2089, culvert, Stebbing Brook, GR 673214. 1865, red brick, two 6ft2in span semicircular arches. Photo p.124.

BRIDGE 2090, underbridge, Mill Lane, GR 676215. 1894 reconstruction, 25ft3in span girders and square trough girder plate flooring, plate sided, red brick abutments. Photo p.124.

BRIDGE 2091, overbridge, 'Lumps', occupation, GR 685216. 1865, yellowish brick, 25ft1in span three-centred arch (p.122).

BRIDGE 2092, overbridge, Watch House (B1417), GR 691217. 1865, red brick, 25ft1in span three-centred arch. Photo above.

BRIDGE 2093, culvert, River Ter, GR 710220. 1865, red brick, 6ft1in span semicircular arch.

BRIDGE 2094, overbridge, Fentons, GR 714221. 1865, red brick, 25ft1in span three-centred arch, skew. Photo above.

RAYNE

Station building/house '1865' 'small' type, 1865, red brick with white brick dressings. House enlarged c1901 (photos pp.22/94/97). WC/coal store lean-to on west side of house (1901?).
Scullery (to west of house) 1865/6, now office.

[All original structures to the east of the main building demolished – the present Gents is a 1994 reconstruction].
[Original platform and rear wall demolished 1994; the present platform and rear wall are new 1994].
[Goods Shed demolished].

Further Reading - P. Paye, The Bishops Stortford Dunmow & Braintree Branch.

BRIDGE 2095, overbridge, Rayne Bridge, GR 731225. 1865, red brick, 25ft2in span three-centred arch. Photo p.24.

BRIDGE 2096, underbridge, 'Clops', occupation, GR 744226. 1865, red brick, 20ft2in span semicircular arch. Photo p.124.

BRIDGE 2097, culvert, River Brain, GR 744226. 1865, red brick, 6ft0in span semicircular arch.

above
The most substantial overbridge on this line is 2079 west of Dunmow which once spanned an open cutting but is now surrounded with trees. This type of bridge with three segmental arches was another standard type on the '1865' lines (although there were no other examples on this line), used for the wider cuttings. The arches are of four rings, and the string course is four courses in width.

above
Semicircular-arch underbridges were built for most occupation roads, this form of arch being possible in such cases because the span required is significantly less than for most public road underbridges. There were five such bridges on this line; 2076 2086 and 2096 remain, 2070 and 2082 are demolished. This is Bridge 2096 which has a relatively wide 20ft 2ins span, in a relatively low embankment, so the arches spring from close to ground level.

above
Only three of the culverts on this line were deemed worthy of numbering by the GER. This is the Stebbing Brook 'bridge' 2089 which is unusually constructed as two parallel tunnels.

left
This view of occupation underbridge 2076 shows well the wing walls which had double-bullnose coping bricks as with the parapet walls. The parapet wall here is a recent rebuild.

Girder underbridges 2072, 2073, 2077 and 2085 (all still extant) were reconstructed in this form with corrugated cross–troughing in 1894/5, to take heavier trains. This is Bridge 2073. They had been cast-iron girder bridges pre-1894 but no photographs of them in their original form are known.

Four other underbridges - 2084, 2088 (now demolished), 2090, and 2099 (now demolished) - were reconstructed at the same time with other types of girder span. 2090, seen here, and 2088 had square trough girder plate flooring and longitudinal running timbers.

21. STANSTED AIRPORT BRANCH

STANSTED AIRPORT

Basement level station, all structures 1990.

22. [ELSENHAM] TO THAXTED

Owing to its 'Light Railway' construction, there are few remains from this line, and most of the trackbed has been eliminated. There are also no remains at any of the intermediate Halts.

SIBLEYS

[No remains]

THAXTED

Station building, timber, 1913.

Loco Shed, red brick, 1913.

Water Tower, red brick base (was used as locomen's mess room) and iron tank, 1913.

(site is visible from public footpath but not accessible).

Further Reading - P. Paye, The Thaxted Branch, OPC, 1984.

Thaxted station building shortly after the opening of the line in 1913. Tenders for the construction of stations/station buildings on the branch were considered in June 1912, and the job was given to William Bell & Son, building contractors of Castle Street, Cambridge, who had submitted the lowest tender at £1,537. The other tenderers were well-known firms of railway contractors, including H.V.Smith & Co who had the main contract for this line. The main building at Sibleys was to the same design but a little shorter. Both stations also had a smaller wooden hut (seen at far right here). The general arrangement of the main building with overhanging roof on the platform side was clearly derived from Tollesbury Pier (p.142), but all the constructional details are different. The GER Engineers Dept must have designed these buildings.

Thaxted loco shed and water tank in 1972, scarcely changed since closure. This is now the only surviving loco shed in Essex. *Geoff Pember*

23. [AUDLEY END] to [BARTLOW]

Current Status of Trackbed

Audley End to Ashdon Road (GR 554389)	Only short sections intact
Ashdon Road to Ashdon Halt (GR 574417)	Largely intact, not accessible
Ashdon Halt to GR 581429	Eliminated
GR 581429 to 'Ashdon Road' track (GR 581435)	Largely intact, not accessible
'Ashdon Road' to county boundary south of Bartlow (GR 585446)	Partly intact, not accessible

BRIDGE 2116, overbridge, Debden Road, GR 538379. 1865, cast iron girder span on red brick abutments. Filled in on west side.

SAFFRON WALDEN

Station building/house, 1865 (see p.20). Recently converted to two houses, with small new canopy added on platform side.

BRIDGE 2117, overbridge, South Road, GR 541380. Western half 1865, 24ft cast iron girder span on brick abutments. Eastern half 1886 when bridge widened, 25ft wrought iron girder span on widened abutments, superstructure modified 1937. Not accessible at formation level and not well seen from road.

ACROW HALT

Concrete platform, 1957.

BRIDGE 2122, overbridge, Butlers Lane alias Painters Bridge, GR 564399. 1866, red brick, three segmental arches (three rings), skew.

ASHDON HALT

Platform, derelict, with GER coach body, derelict (five-compartment Second No.342 of 1883, moved to Ashdon 1916).

BRIDGE 2126, overbridge, Ashdon Road, GR 581435. 1866, red brick (white brick arch, blue brick string course, yellow brick parapet walls). 24ft span 3 ring segmental arch, skew. Not accessible at formation level and not well seen from road. Photo at Paye p.62.

Further Reading re this line - P. Paye, The Saffron Walden Branch, OPC, 1981.

Detail of the quoins, with 'nailhead' decoration, Saffron Walden station building.

The Railway Arms Inn at Saffron Walden, situated in Station Road opposite the station, provides the unusual case of a non-railway building based on a railway station. No specific formal connection with the Saffron Walden Railway company is known but no doubt there were personal connections, and one guesses that J.S. Pierce was the architect.

24. [UPMINSTER] TO SHOEBURYNESS

The new 1962 up side Boooking Hall at Benfleet.

above The 1897 up side buildings at Leigh old station are very much in the style of Westcliff, but the plan is very different – the Leigh site is very constricted, and there is no two-storey Station Master's house section here. The brickwork here has not been cleaned. The windows, and the two string courses through and immediately above them, are much as per those in the single storey section of Westcliff, but because the Leigh building is set higher above road level there is another string course here (three courses of red brick) below the windows. The canopy above the 'porch' entrance is in the same vein as those at Woodgrange Park and Dagenham Dock. The portion of the building which now has the flat roof originally sported one gable with corbelled verges in the usual LT&S fashion.

left Detail of window at Westcliff. Note the two different types of shaped red bricks used for the string courses. The keystones at Westcliff are differently-patterned to those at Leigh.

below Looking into Westcliff station through Valkyrie Road bridge on 22.12.1957, with early pre-electrification work in progress. The original down side buildings are glimpsed to the left of the DMU. The additional section of up platform canopy has valancing to match the 1895 canopy sections. *Frank Church*

WEST HORNDON

Station building/house 1886 (see p.59). All in original condition except road side canopy has replacement plain valancing. [Down platform canopy removed].

1993 shelter on up platform. [1886 up platform shelter/canopy removed].

Footbridge, concrete, 1957 (see p.109 note).

LAINDON

Station building/house 1888 (see p.59). House section remains in original condition; Booking Office/Hall section internally rebuilt and extended on road side c1960.

Down platform canopy 1888 (photo p.59), replacement plain valancing.

Up island platform building and canopy steelwork 1933/4, but c1993 the building was reconstructed with new gabled roof, and all the canopy roofing replaced; also a new glass-sided waiting area constructed at west end.

Footbridge, concrete, 1958.

BASILDON

Street level concourse/lift towers/platform canopies 1974.

PITSEA

New main building 2005.

Footbridge between main building and Upminster line platforms 1888 (photo p.60); covering removed.

Footbridge at east end of platforms 1958, concrete.

Footbridge between main building and Tilbury line platforms c1980.

Waiting shelter on Down Upminster line platform 1888, canopy removed.

Signal Box, 1960, BR(ER) Type 18 box, disused (photo p.69).

1887/8 retaining wall behind west end of Down Upminster line platform, also lesser walls behind west ends of Up Upminster and Down Tilbury platforms.

Further Reading – LT&SR Vol.1 pp.66-67.

BENFLEET

Buildings behind up and down platforms, Station Master's house section, and up and down platform canopies, all 1911 (photos p.63). c2000 the house was rewindowed and the passenger entrance area altered.

Additional Booking Hall on up side, 1962.

Bridge over Ferry Road (originally over Benfleet Creek), GR 777859. Three lattice girder spans, carrying station platforms.

Further Reading – LT&SR Vol.2 pp.124-125.

LEIGH-ON-SEA

Main building at road level 1933.

Down platform canopy 1933; only a short section at the east end remains. [1933 buildings behind down platform demolished].

Up platform canopy 1933, widened to south 1955 when the platform became an island. Reduced in length at west end. Up platform building 1933 (photo p.71), rewindowed c2000.

LEIGH OLD STATION

1897 up side buildings, yellow brick with red brick dressings, two hipped roof sections plus further section to east altered with new flat roof. Now occupied by Leigh-on-Sea Sailing Club, exterior remains in largely original condition.

Further Reading – Midland Record No.16.

CHALKWELL

Main building (at road level) 1933, similar to Leigh-on-Sea. Doors/windows mostly new.

Steel footbridge (plate-sided, covered) and covered stairs to platforms 1933.

400ft up platform canopy and up platform buildings 1933, fully intact.

200ft down platform canopy and down platform buildings 1933, fully intact. Windows in platform buildings have horizontal glazing bars only.

Full height yellow brick wall behind up platform 1933.

BRIDGE 237, overbridge, Valkyrie Road, GR 866855. 1903/4 (contract to Mowlem May 1903). Unique bridge, iron segmental arch with yellow brick above. Photo p.126.

The down platform range at Chalkwell; all doors and windows are original.

Chalkwell footbridge. This has much in common with the footbridges at the other LMS-built LT&S line stations, but they vary according to the position of the station entrance building. The covering is timber-built and has windows with horizontal glazing bars only.

WESTCLIFF

Station buildings/house 1894/5, see p.61.

Single-storey Booking Office building at east end 1961, burnt out c1990, rebuilt internally and reopened 1993.

Up platform canopy 1894/5, full length remains. 'LT&SR' type brackets (see p.61). Longitudinal and transverse girders at same height. Late C20 plain valancing.

Separate length of open canopy on up platform between Valkyrie Road bridge and footbridge, c1900-10, valancing replaced c1960.

Down side canopy is 1980s reconstruction using original columns and 'LT&SR' brackets. Small brick 1980s building under this canopy.

Footbridge, concrete, 1958.

BRIDGE 243, overbridge, Milton Road, GR 873854. Western half of bridge original, three segmental arches. Eastern half is c1960 widening, concrete span.

SOUTHEND CENTRAL

Station buildings 1889, red brick (contract to Lucas & Aird 22.11.1888 at £17,619). Platform canopies also 1889 except as noted below. See pp.60-61. [The following 1889 sections are now demolished – porte-cochere over up side entrance, western half of platforms 1/2 canopy, short section at west end of platforms 3/4 canopy, detached Station Master's house].

Additional north-south concourse area (at west end of 1889 up side buildings) 1899, in same style. Contract to Mowlem. [Provided to serve the additional platforms 5/6, now removed]. Platforms 3/4 canopy widened 1899, see p.61.

Signal Box 1960, BR(ER) Type 18 box, now staff accommodation.

'Central House', BR office block, c1960.

Lengthy boundary wall (red brick) along north side of Scratton Road, 1899?

Further Reading – LT&SR Vol.1 pp.34-37.

BRIDGE 268, overbridge, Chase Road, GR 893857. Western half of bridge is original, 1884, three segmental arches. Eastern half is c1960 widening, concrete span.

SOUTHEND EAST

[1932 main building on south side, and the whole of the south side platform, demolished].

Small B.O. building at street level on north side, c1990.

The up side Waiting Room at Chalkwell retains a full set of original benches.

Doorway between the Booking Hall and platform 3.

The wall of the 1899 section of concourse facing Scratton Road.

Canopy detail on platform 2, showing one of the columns with longitudinal as well as transverse brackets, the latter slightly larger. It is not clear why some columns have four brackets and others only two. The three-branch decoration on the capitals should be compared with Laindon (p.59).

Window in the 1889 up side frontage.

above left
Detail of brickwork, up side.

above right
The 1889 Booking Hall ceiling, showing the star decoration on the capitals of the pilasters supporting the trussed girders.

right
Detail of the down side porte-cochere at Southend Central. The valancing at this station is not the same as that at the 1885-93 new lines stations. Note how the boards in the curved sections are cut non-symmetrically to produce a proper semi-circular cut-out in each case.

Station footbridge, 1932, covered, with brick-built covered staircase on down platform and steel column supports to up side covered staircase.

Public footbridge (on east side of station footbridge) 1932.

Up platform (which was originally middle island platform) has standard LMS LT&S section island platform type canopy with two rows of plain steel columns and skylighting. Reduced in length at east and west ends.

Up platform building 1932, small-pane windows.

Signal box relay room, c1960, red brick, on down platform. [Signal Box demolished].

[The down platform never had any other building, or canopy].

THORPE BAY

Station buildings/house 1910, yellow brick with red brick dressings, see p.62. Contract to Charles Wall 13.1.1910 at £7,750.

Up side buildings and up platform canopy are fully intact (but house section is boarded up).

1910 down side building and canopy also intact, canopy extended eastwards in same style 1912.

Footbridge, concrete, c1959.

Further Reading – LT&SR Vol.2 pp.113-114.

SHOEBURYNESS

Station building 1884, with unknown alterations after 1891 fire. See p.58.

Platform canopy 1884 (?), cut back in width 1980s.

Small brick entrance porch on road side, pre-1896.

25. PURFLEET TO [PITSEA]

PURFLEET

Station building c1960, white brick, flat roof.

Footbridge, concrete, c1960.

GRAYS

Station building (up side) c1955, yellow brick, flat concrete roof.

Down platform building 1980s.

Station Master's house ('Station House') c1880s.

Footbridge at level crossing, 1884?, replacement span c1960, boarded off.

TILBURY TOWN

Station building (up side) 1998, red brick, gabled roof.

Down platform building 1998.

Footbridge, steel, 1998.

TILBURY RIVERSIDE

(All buildings and structures 1926-30, see pp.70-71).

Station concourse, incorporating roof from 1906 concourse. Boarded off, no access.

PLA Baggage Hall, now 'London International Cruise Terminal', refurbished 1985. Photo p.71.

Office block to east side of station concourse, now 'Tilbury Riverside Arts Activity Centre'.

Floating Landing Stage and connecting bridges, opened 1928. Vehicle bridge at east end is used for public access to ferry, no access to other areas.

LOW STREET

Goods Shed, 1861.

EAST TILBURY

Station building 1984, yellow brick with red brick dressings. (Concrete station platforms also 1984).

Muckingford Crossing crossing house, 1854, the last survivor of the original LT&S line crossing houses (for which see LT&SR Vol.1 p.20), but so much altered as to be unrecognisable.

STANFORD-LE-HOPE

Station building c1960.

Platform shelters 1991.

Footbridge, concrete, 1959.

26. [UPMINSTER] to [GRAYS]

OCKENDON

Station building/house 1892. House section rewindowed. [Canopy over entrance on road side removed].

[Down platform canopy removed].

Up platform shelter 1892, standard new lines type, the only intact example. Retains valancing on front only.

Footbridge, concrete, 1957.

BRIDGE 25, STIFFORD VIADUCT, GR 591801. Fourteen segmental arches. Photos p.63 and below.

CHAFFORD HUNDRED

Station building 1995.

27. THAMES HAVEN BRANCH

BRIDGE 2, underbridge, Mucking Creek, GR 686817. c1944, concrete.

THAMES HAVEN

Inspector's Office, 1953, brick, single storey, with timber built second floor 1964.

Further Reading – P. Kay, The Thames Haven Railway, 1999.

Mucking Creek bridge. The rebuilding of this bridge was enforced by the heavier trains using the Thames Haven branch in the latter part of the war.

Ockendon Road bridge at North Ockendon (GR 581851) in May 1958. This type of three-arch segmental arch overbridge was common on the 1885-93 new lines, but almost all (including this one) had the centre arch replaced by a concrete span, and the side arches bricked up, in the pre-electrification works.

Frank Church

below

A different view of Stifford Viaduct - captured by Frank Church on 11th May 1958, looking north. As is very evident here the viaduct was built for double track.

Frank Church

28. [CHAPPEL] TO [HAVERHILL]

Current Status of Trackbed

Chappel to GR 884295	Largely eliminated
GR 884295 to White Colne Station LC (GR 871291)	Largely intact, not accessible
White Colne Station LC to Colne Park Road (GR 868293)	Cutting intact, de facto footpath along north side of cutting
Colne Park Road to River Colne bridge (GR 856297)	Intact, official footpath (not shown by OS as such)
River Colne bridge to White's bridges (GR 846297)	Largely eliminated
White's bridges to Langley Mill LC	Largely intact, not accessible
Langley Mill LC to GR 830300	Intact, de facto footpath
GR 830300 to GR 822300	Intact, not accessible
GR 822300 to Parsonage Street (GR 816302)	Intact, walkable on formation or either side
Parsonage Street LC to Trinity Street LC (Halstead Yard)	Much built on, no through access, but coal yard at Parsonage Street end still clear
Trinity Street LC to GR 810307	Eliminated, car park etc
GR 810307 to A1124 (GR 804318)	Intact, trackbed itself not walkable but footpaths on one or the other side
A1124 to GR 784343	Largely intact, not accessible
Sible Hedingham station site, GR 784343 to GR 781348	Eliminated
GR 781348 to GR 778358	Largely intact, not accessible
GR 778358 to GR 769364	COLNE VALLEY RAILWAY
GR 769364 to GR 760378	Partly intact (cutting at Lark Hill Farm largely filled in, embankment either side of River Colne at GR 760377 intact except for river crossing itself).
Yeldham station site	Eliminated
GR 758382 to GR 756385	Intact, not accessible
GR 756385 to GR 752387	Intact, public footpath
GR 752387 to GR 740394	Mostly intact
GR 740394 to GR 735398	Mostly eliminated
GR 735398 to GR 727404	Partly intact
GR 727404 to GR 723408	Mostly eliminated
GR 723408 to GR 696432	Mostly intact
GR 696432 to present county boundary at Haverhill Bypass (GR 683442)	Largely eliminated

BRIDGE No.1, overbridge, Station Road, GR 897294. 1859. Photo p.65.

FOX & PHEASANT CROSSING (Boley Road, GR 897291). Crossing house, single storey, dated 1880.

WHITE COLNE

Station building 1860, extended 1908, see p.64.

EARLS COLNE

Station building / house 1904/5, see p.65. House section extended 1990s in same style.

1882 timber station building now in builders yard at Colne Engaine, see p.64.

LANGLEY MILL CROSSING. Crossing house to NE of level crossing at GR 837298. C17 house rented by the railway, restored after bomb damage 1940 and much extended late C20.

PARSONAGE LANE CROSSING (actually Parsonage Street, GR 816302). Crossing house, LNER, 1930. See p.65.

HALSTEAD

Workshops building on south side of Factory Lane West, c1890s.
Water tank base, yellow brick, with shed and office buildings attached.

The Corn Exchange alias Market House (now library) was not a railway building but the CV&HR rented it for some years as a storage shed.

HULLS MILL BRIDGE, overbridge, GR 793333. Brick arch, hardly visible from road.

ALDERFORD STREET BRIDGE, overbridge, GR 787341. Brick arch, hardly visible from road.

RELICS OF THE CV&HR

right Fox & Pheasant Crossing cottage.

middle The sole surviving Halstead workshops building.

bottom The water tank base at Halstead. The gabled red brick office building to its left (windows now bricked up) served latterly as the SM's office; the brick shed to its right was used as the P.Way Trolley Shed.

The real Halstead station building, which was demolished some years after closure. It was designed by Joseph Cubitt and erected in 1862. Apart from the fact that it was built of the same Suffolk stock blocks, it had nothing in common with the White Colne and Sible & Castle Hedingham buildings.

Graham Austin collection

above

Sible & Castle Hedingham station building in situ in the 1920s. It was identical to the White Colne building (p.64) – until extended in 1908 the latter also had the same lean-to section at the near end, and a similar small canopy (see photo in *British Railway Journal* No.39 p.399). Both were built of offwhite 'Suffolk stock' blocks manufactured in Sudbury (much larger than ordinary bricks), with red brick dressings.

Graham Austin collection

right

The Sible & Castle Hedingham building as seen today re-erected at the Colne Valley Railway site. (For the corresponding end of the White Colne building see p.64). The platform side, and both ends, of the building were carefully rebuilt in their original state, but the road side was made quite different and is faced in ordinary white bricks.

SIBLE & CASTLE HEDINGHAM

[No remains].

COLNE VALLEY RAILWAY SITE

Station building from Sible & Castle Hedingham (1861) re-erected here on north side platform 1975-6.

Building on south side platform built 1977-9 using salvaged parts from Halstead, Sible Hedingham, and St Ives, plus canopy columns and brackets from Glemsford, also bricks from Yeldham goods shed (granary) which was dismantled 1975. The CVR also had to have some new Suffolk stock blocks made to erect this building as there were insufficient available second-hand. However the largely-unseen rear of this building is in modern red brick throughout.

This building (photo p.110) is referred to as 'Halstead' by the CVR purely for operating convenience, from which a mistaken idea has arisen that it is a direct rebuild of the original Halstead building, to which it bears no resemblance.

'Hedingham' signal box is Cressing SB top (GER Type 7, 1891) on new brick base (1980). McKenzie & Holland 1886 Patent 5in frame, 20 levers, 1891, ex Cressing.

'Nunnery Junction' signal box is Wrabness SB top (GER Type 1, 1875 – see p.68) on new brick base (c1985). Saxby & Farmer Rocker frame, 25 levers, date n/k, ex Wrabness.

Ground frame / lamp room brick hut ex White Colne (1908?), re-erected here 1976 (adjacent to 'Hedingham' signal box).

Footbridge from Stowmarket, 1898 there, re-erected here 1982. 'A.Handyside & Co Ltd 1898 Derby & London' maker's plates.

BRIDGE No.19, underbridge, River Colne (adjacent to 'Hedingham' signal box). Girders second hand from White's bridge No.1 west of Earls Colne, 1908/9 there, re-erected here by CVR on original Bridge 19 brick abutments.

BRIDGE, overbridge, GR 762373. Largely filled in.

YELDHAM

[No remains].

BRIDGE, overbridge, GR 720414 (Birdbrook cutting). Segmental arch.

BIRDBROOK

Goods Shed, c1900, much altered.

Pair of cottages, c1905. Not certain that these were actually built by the CV&HR directly, but they were at least arranged to be built for the CV&HR's use.

Further Reading – GE Journal 123.

Further Reading for Colne Valley line generally – The Colne Valley & Halstead Railway, R.A. Whitehead and F.D.Simpson, 2nd edition, Oakwood Press 1987; From Construction to Destruction, An Authentic History of the Colne Valley and Halstead Railway, E.P.Willingham, 1989; British Railway Journal No.39.

---

29. CORRINGHAM LIGHT RAILWAY

Current Status of Trackbed
(on lifted section)

Corringham station (GR 713838) to GR 720833
Largely intact, part walkable

GR 720833 to triangular junction at GRs 733824/735826
Largely eliminated

CORRINGHAM

[No remains].

CORYTON

Brick platform (the western end of the reconstructed platform of c1915).

Further Reading - I.Gotheridge, The Corringham Light Railway, Oakwood Press, 1985.

MANGAPPS FARM

(near Burnham on Crouch, GR 944980).

The following structures have been re-erected at this site:

Station building from Horham, Mid Suffolk Light Railway. c1905, standard MSLR timber-framed building with corrugated iron cladding. (At 'Mangapps' station).

Ground frame hut from Billericay, 1937, timber, gabled. (First Class Waiting Room).

Waiting Hut plus canopy from Brampton. Originally at Great Ormesby M&GN, 1894; moved to Brampton 1960.

Midland Railway lamp hut from Westcliff LT&SR.

Signal Box from Berney Arms, GER non-standard ground level timber box, 1885. 4-lever ground frame from another location.

GER hut, formerly signalman's toilet at Edmonton Junction.

Haddiscoe Junction signal box ('Mangapps Junction'), GER Type 7 box, 1904. Previously at Science Museum South Kensington until 1996. Reduced in length. [Frame from this box is still at Science Museum].

Goods Yard crane from Ruskington, GN&GE Joint.

Station building from Laxfield, Mid Suffolk Light Railway. c1905, same type as Horham. (At 'Old Heath' station).

APPENDIX: ESSEX STATION BUILDINGS NO LONGER EXTANT

The listing here is in line order as per the Gazetteer in the main part of this volume. The list refers to the *principal* building at each station; subsidiary buildings are (with one exception) not covered here. The building date only is given except in cases where there were two or more consecutive buildings, in which case demolition dates are given as well. At the end of the Appendix the major demolished viaducts in Essex are also illustrated.

* indicates that the building is illustrated in these volumes, either in this Appendix or (where so noted) elsewhere.

Brentwood 1840-1845 temporary station — No views known

*Brentwood 1845-1932 main building (up side)

Shenfield 1847-1850 station — No views known

*Shenfield 1886-1932 street level buildings

Shenfield 1933-c1970 street level building — (Photo in British Railways Illustrated Annual no.5)

Ingatestone 1844-1846 temporary buildings — No views known (timber?)

Chelmsford 1843-1856 station — No views known (except for views of one of the platform buildings as re-erected in Broomfield Road, see GE Journal 33)

*Chelmsford 1856-1987 main building (up side) — See photo p.85

Hatfield Peverel 1844/5-1849 station — No views known (timber)

*Witham 1843-1906 main building (timber)

Kelvedon 1843-1871 buildings — No views known (timber)

*Kelvedon 1871-1990 main building

Marks Tey 1844/5-1864 station — No views known (except for the poor view of the platform shelters at p.169 of Joby, *The Eastern Counties Railway)*

*Marks Tey 1864-c1973 main building (up side) — See photo p.96

*Colchester 1843 buildings (timber, some lasted until 1895) The history of this station has yet to be properly researched

Colchester 1865-1960 main down side building. — Only partial views known

*Ardleigh 1846 (EUR)

Manningtree 1846-1899 buildings (EUR) — No views known

Loughton 1856-1865 station (timber) — No views known For a detailed description see H.W. Paar, *Loughton's First Railway Station*

*Loughton 1865-1940 station — See photo p.96

*Battlesbridge 1889

*Woodham Ferrers 1889

Fambridge 1889 — As Althorne

*Althorne 1889

*Cold Norton 1889

*Maldon West 1889

*Braintree 1848-1869 station

Tiptree 1904, Tolleshunt D'Arcy 1904, Tollesbury 1904 — Identical Light Railway type small timber buildings, see P. Paye, *The Tollesbury Branch*

*Tollesbury Pier 1907

*Bures 1849 (EUR)

Wivenhoe 1863-1886 buildings (THR) — No views known but almost certainly of the standard THR type

*Thorington 1866 (THR)

*Clacton 1882-1929 buildings

Brightlingsea 1866-1901 station (W&BR) — No views known, timber with trainshed roof

Brightlingsea 1906 station — See Paye pp. 36, 49, 58

*Bradfield date nk

*Wrabness 1854 (EUR) — See photo p.17

*Harwich 1854-1866 station (EUR)

Burnt Mill date nk — Small single storey brick building, see photo GE Journal 87.37. Demolished c1959.

Sawbridgeworth 1841 main building (N&ER). — Two-storey brick house with semicircular- arched windows, unlike any other known N&ER building. Demolished 1960s. No good views known.

Sawbridgeworth 1865-196x main building — Timber, hipped, single storey

Spelbrook 1841 temporary terminus (N&ER) — No views known

Bishops Stortford 1842-1845 station (N&ER) — Timber, trainshed roof. See p.2 of P. Paye, *The Bishops Stortford Dunmow and Braintree Branch*

*Dunmow 1865 — See photo p.95

Sibleys 1913 — Similar to Thaxted, photos in P. Paye, *The Thaxted Branch*

Pitsea 1855-1888 station — No views known

Pitsea 1888-196x main building — See photo at Dow, *London Tilbury & Southend Album*, p.28.

Pitsea 196x-2005 main building

Benfleet 1855-1901 main building (up side) — No views known

Benfleet 1901 -1911 temporary building (up side) — Shack - see photo at Dow p.76 upper

Leigh 1855-1897 main building (up side) — See photo at Dow p. 12

*Southend [Central] 1856-1889 buildings

Southend East 1932 main building (up side) — LMS standard type

Purfleet Rifle Range 1911 — Large timber sheds, no good views

Purfleet 1854-196x main building (upside)

Grays 1854-1884 main building (up side) — Photo at Dow p.9

Grays 1884-c1955 main building (up side) — Photo at Dow p.69

Tilbury Town 1886-1964 main building (up side)

Tilbury Town 1964-1998 main building (up side)

Tilbury Riverside 1854-1906 buildings

Tilbury Riverside 1906-1928 buildings — Photo at Dow p.71

Low Street 1861 — Small single-storey brick building, see photo at LT&SR Vol.1 p.33

Stanford-le-Hope 1854-c1920 main building — See photo at LT&SR Vol.1 p.21

Stanford-le-Hope c1920-c1960 main building — See photo at Dow p.40 upper

Thames Haven 1855 building — See photos in *The Thames Haven Railway*

*Halstead 1862

Yeldham 1862? — Small single-storey timber buildings, best views in *British Railway Journal* 39

Birdbrook 1863? Ditto

above

A view of the 1843-1906 main (up side) building at Witham, which ended up as the last survivor of the 1843 'temporary' Colchester line timber buildings.

The Board decided on 7.7.1842 (at a stage when it was expected to open to Colchester in September 1842) that only temporary station buildings should be provided, as cheap as possible. £100 was allocated for Ingatestone [i.e. Stock Lane], £2000 for Chelmsford, £500 for Witham, £300 for Kelvedon, and £2000 for Colchester. Grissell & Peto were appointed as contractors. In October 1842 Braithwaite reported that the stations at Chelmsford, Witham, Kelvedon and Colchester were almost completed. [Shenfield, Hatfield Peverel, and Marks Tey were not original 1843 stations].

A new road (now Easton Road) was built by the ECR from Braintree Road as the access to this building. The 1843 down side building was separately accessed via another new road, now Albert Road.

John Palombi collection

above

This view of the old Colchester up side building is perhaps well-known, but there has been no previous comment on the construction. In fact if one takes away the 1860s-style GER road side canopy, it will be seen that the building is virtually as Witham, thereby confirming it as the original 1843 building (as is also suggested by maps).

right

The 1845 main building at Brentwood in its original state. Most of the large finials were later removed, and a flat awning was added above the three entrance archways. This drawing appears to be accurate apart from the usual propensity of early Victorian artists to exaggerate the verticals.

It is difficult to see that anybody other than Sancton Wood could have been responsible for the Brentwood buildings; this is confirmed by a Traffic Committee minute of 24.2.1847 which records a payment of balance to him 'for superintending works at Brentwood'. The building has much in common with the station building at Peterborough East which was also under construction in summer 1845, although it is unclear whether Sancton Wood or Livock was responsible there.

bottom right

There is no known record as to why Braintree did not receive a grand terminus like Maldon's in 1847/8. This 24ft by 8ft ECR timber building was no doubt meant to be 'temporary', but it lasted in passenger use until the new station on the Bishops Stortford line opened in 1869, and continued after that as a goods yard office, not being demolished until 1997. The left hand section was the Station Master's office, the central portion the Booking Hall, and the right hand side Booking Office plus storeroom. The Booking Hall led to a steep flight of stairs down to the platform. Photograph c1925.

above

The original EUR stations of 1846 (Ardleigh, Manningtree (? - no photos known), Bentley, and the original Ipswich terminus) were erected by the Ipswich contractor Samuel Baldiston; more detailed analysis is perhaps best left to a more EUR-related work. Ardleigh is seen here in the 1920s. Here and at Bentley there were also quite-unrelated two-storey crossing houses with very fancy bargeboards. (Ardleigh's is demolished but Bentley's survives, much altered). At left is the Saxby & Farmer-built GER Type 1 signal box dating back to the installation of block in the 1870s.

Graham Austin collection

right

The 1854 Harwich station was entirely timber-built, perhaps because the ground was new-made (there was no likelihood at the time of the station having to be only temporary). The elaborate decoration confirms an intention of permanence. The same form of bargeboard decoration was found on the 1854 goods shed (left) and the 1853 Halfpenny Pier Booking Office.

right

(See also front cover photo). When the Sudbury line opened in 1849, Bures was the only station with a substantial building. The line was on embankment at this point so the building was of three storeys. The first/second floor windows on the road side are in the same vein as the contemporary Barnes building at Mellis (*cf* also the later Mistley and Harleston). There are also affinities between Bures and the much smaller house at Mount Bures Crossing (p.53). The date of the platform canopy with its non-standard struts has not been established, but c1890 is most likely. One imagines that the northern half of the platform was originally timber-built. At right is the hut which survives today. The main building was demolished in 1973.

Graham Austin collection

above and right It is not at all evident why Thorington station was not built to the same standard style as most of the other Tendring Hundred Railway stations. There are certainly no site constraints, and it did open with the line. It was not a place likely to be seen as needing a larger building because of heavy traffic! The design is effectively a blown-up version of the Norwich & Spalding / Waveney Valley / Frinton type gatehouses (see p.20).

The road side view, dating from the 1920s, shows the new flatroofed Booking Office extension made in 1891 to give a passenger entrance separate from the house. The other flat-roof section may also have been added at this date but maps are unhelpful. The wooden gatekeeper's hut at left (the only structure in these views that survives in 2007) probably dates from 1883, starting life as a temporary Block Telegraph Hut when block working was brought into use on this line prior to the erection of interlocked signal boxes. The 'notched' bargeboards, similar to those on GER Type 2 signal boxes, add to the likelihood of such a date. Thorington subsequently acquired a *second* hut of this type (right), perhaps second-hand from one of the other stations on this line.

The platform view, looking down line from the level crossing, shows clearly the join in the brickwork between the original building and the 1891 Booking Office section.

The brick-built Gents half way along the platform survived until recent years for the Crossing Keeper's use, but has now gone.

The down platform was added in 1885 when the station became a passing place. It had a Waiting Room block of the Weeley type which survived derelict until 2006.

The Lens of Sutton collection / Graham Austin collection

bottom right [An exception to our 'principal buildings only' rule!]. The up platform Waiting Room block at Weeley, provided in 1884 when Weeley became a passing place. Thorington (1885) and Hythe (1886) also had buildings to this design, which seems to have been evolved by Ashbee for the Mildenhall branch (examples at Barnwell Junction, Bottisham, Burwell, Isleham). It is decidedly different in spirit from most Ashbee buildings. Several had brick bases, at least latterly.

Graham Austin collection

top

The 1882 Clacton station building was the last to be built in Essex by a small local GER constituent company. Bruff was presumably responsible for this unusual all-timber design. The Refreshment Room block was added by the GER in 1886, the contract being given to W.T.Hook on 6.4.1886 at £439. The original Refreshment Room was given over to a Booking Office extension. The new 1929 main building was erected largely in front of the old buildings.

Graham Austin collection

middle

Bradfield was not an original station, but was opened at an unknown date c1856. It is not proven that the building dates from the station's opening, although it can hardly be later than the mid 1860s given its appearance. It is in a style of its own so far as ECR/GER station buildings go. The road side has Tudoresque features in the form of doorways with four-centred arches and windows with hood moulds.

Graham Austin collection

bottom

The 1871 Kelvedon building in the 1920s, with the entrance canopy under repair. The GER had received a complaint in August 1870 from Sir T.B. Western MP about the continued existence of the 1843 'temporary' building. This brought immediate action, with plans for a new building being approved in September, and the contract being given to O.T.Gibbons in March 1871 at £770. The building has some commonality of spirit with the new Kings Lynn station also built in 1871, and must be attributed to the then GER Engineer Henry W. Davis. At right is the later Station Master's house.

Graham Austin collection

right

Shenfield (the second station) was built in 1886 in preparation for the opening of the New Essex lines, and was the first complete station in Essex to the new Ashbee style. The site dictated an abnormal plan - the main range was behind the down platform, but the SM's house and a small entrance hall were set at road level at an angle to the platforms. The building seen above the entrance here is the rear of the signal box. The entrance has a flat canopy as Frinton. The house section has its upper storey rendered but one cannot be sure that this was originally so.

below

Woodham Ferrers, February 1966. This station was of the Rochford/Southminster type, 'handed' the same way as Southminster. The flat canopy that these stations had above the entrance is again similar to Frinton's. The near end of the building was demolished in 1968. At left is the goods lock-up, of the usual New Lines type, *cf* Hockley.

G.L.Pring / Railway Record of the British Isles

above

The house section at Woodham Ferrers survived longer, and is seen here in June 1973. Compare Southminster p.33.

right

The north end of the Southminster building, prior to the 1968 demolitions when the 'pavilion' and everything to its left went.

G.L. Pring / Railway Record of the British Isles

above

Battlesbridge, seen here on 6th February 1966, and Cold Norton (below) were, as noted at p.34, to the same design and plan (and 'handed' the same way as) Hockley and Prittlewell.

G.L.Pring / Railway Record of the British Isles

below

Cold Norton, date unknown (the station buildings were demolished in 1954). Here there was a standard goods lock-up, but Battlesbridge did not have one as it was provided with a goods shed.

Graham Austin collection

left

Althorne (as noted at p.30) was a copy of Wivenhoe, but in the absence of an attached house section there was a tiled-gable east end. The station is seen in the cold weather of February 1963.

John Watling

Maldon West's unique street level building (1889) housed the Booking Office only. The steeply-pitched roof was provided with a window in the left-hand gable. The wall at left fronted the Station Master's garden (see map p.102).

Graham Austin collection

Not a 'demolished station'! - but a 1920s view of Witham with its original canopy that has only come to light since the publication of the first volume.

Graham Austin collection

above

A 1920s view of the Tollesbury Pier station building and wooden platform. The building can never have seen much use and would have been unused for traffic purposes after the closure of the Tollesbury - Tollesbury Pier section in 1921, hence the boarded-up doors.

Graham Austin collection

left

The building at Burwarton on the Cleobury Mortimer & Ditton Priors Light Railway, seen when new in 1908. Of the four buildings on the CM&DPLR, Cleobury Town, Stottesdon, and Ditton Priors were 'handed' the same way as Tollesbury Pier, whereas Burwarton was handed the other way.

below

As one of the major demolished GER structures in Essex, Tollesbury Pier itself deserves illustrating here. This 1920s view appears to have been taken from the middle steps. There are no known close views of the rather small 50ft by 18ft pierhead area.

Graham Austin collection

TOLLESBURY PIER

The Tollesbury - Tollesbury Pier extension, constructed in 1906/7, was engineered by John Wilson's son Edward A.Wilson who had joined the company staff in 1892 and in fact became 'Assistant Engineer' in 1907. The pier itself was of course the major work on the extension. The Tollesbury Pier station building was the only building involved. It may be guessed that E.A. Wilson and his staff designed it without Ashbee becoming involved! The 1904 station buildings on the original portion of the Tollesbury branch were to a different design without the overhanging eaves (albeit they too were gabled timber buildings with corrugated iron roofing). Perhaps there had been complaints from passengers or staff about the lack of protection from driving rain at the 1904 stations?

The contractors for the Extension were Messrs Bott & Stennett, a partnership formed in 1899 between Arthur F. Bott and William Stennett (and dissolved in 1908). Whilst working on the Tollesbury Pier line they obtained in September 1906 the contract for building the Cleobury Mortimer & Ditton Priors Light Railway. Bott & Stennett's Engineer on the CM&DPLR, Walter Atkinson, had as one of his Assistant Engineers Herbert Wilson, E.A. Wilson's brother - a position which he may have got thanks to the contacts made at Tollesbury. Atkinson kept a diary in which he recorded how John Wilson made a visit to Cleobury Mortimer and 'imparted some fatherly advice' to Herbert. The drawings for the Tollesbury Pier station building must have also made their way to the CM&DPLR Engineer's office, and were used for the erection of four station buildings on that line.

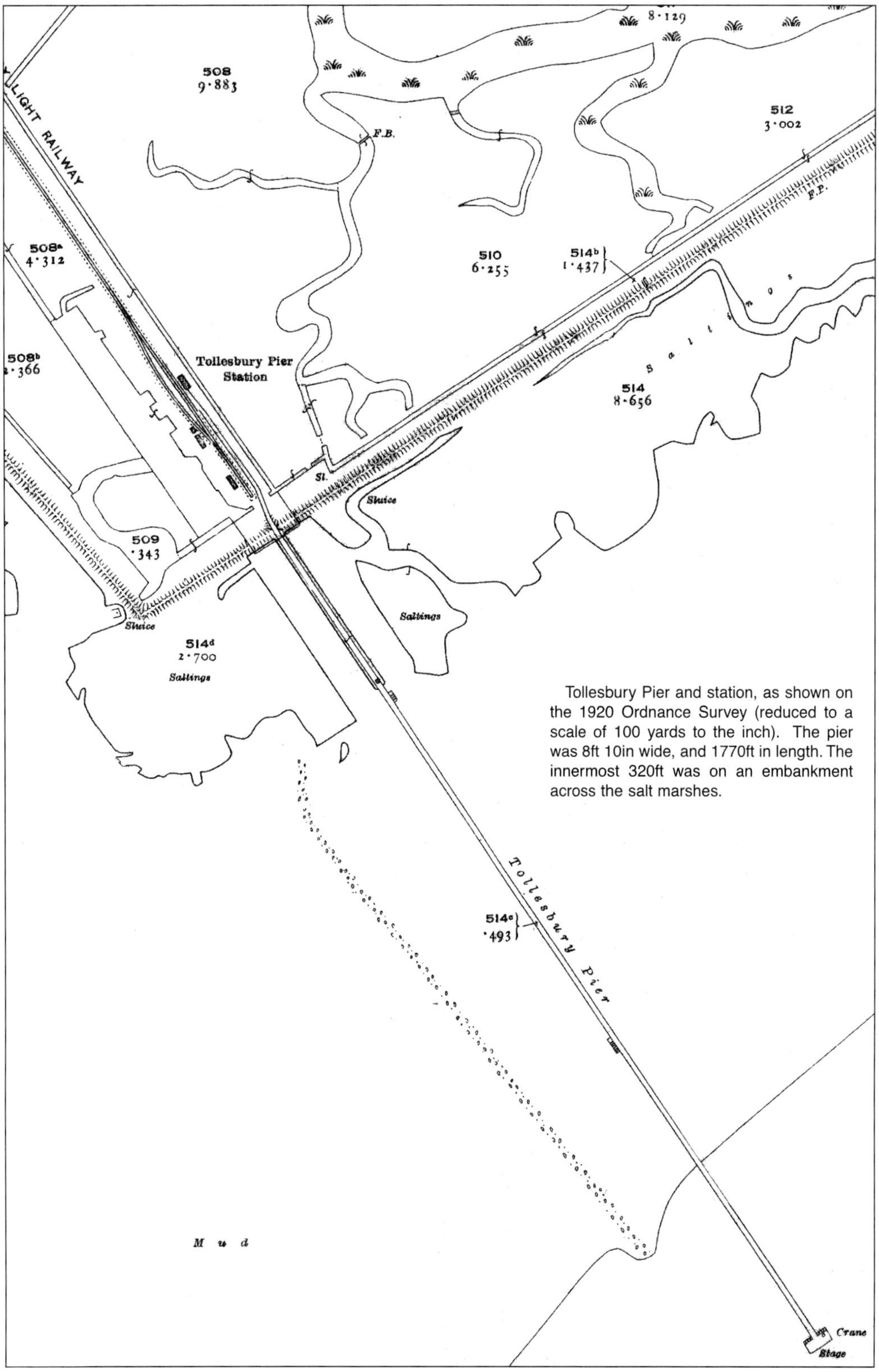

Tollesbury Pier and station, as shown on the 1920 Ordnance Survey (reduced to a scale of 100 yards to the inch). The pier was 8ft 10in wide, and 1770ft in length. The innermost 320ft was on an embankment across the salt marshes.

The remains of Tollesbury Pier today - just portions of the timber palisading that protected the embankment on the marshes. The main timber section of the pier lasted into the 1950s (apart from a short section removed for anti-invasion reasons in 1940) but had been in gradual decay since the 1920s.

A present day view of the site of Tollesbury Pier station looking NW from the sea wall with the intact trackbed stretching away towards Tollesbury in the distance.

The 1856-1889 LT&SR station at Southend had some of the most substantial station buildings ever erected in Essex - a 220ft by 45ft trainshed roof and a 140ft long brick range along the south side. The east end of the trainshed was open until 1881 when the large porte-cochere seen here was provided in connection with the holding of the Essex Show in Southend that year. Unfortunately it had to be taken down again in 1882 for the start of work on the Shoeburyness extension. For more on this station see LT&SR Vol.1 pp. 34-37.

Other Essex stations with trainshed roofs were the Bishops Stortford 1842-5 temporary station; the first Tilbury station of 1854-1906; the 1855 Thames Haven station; and the first Brightlingsea station of 1866-1901.

DEMOLISHED ESSEX VIADUCTS

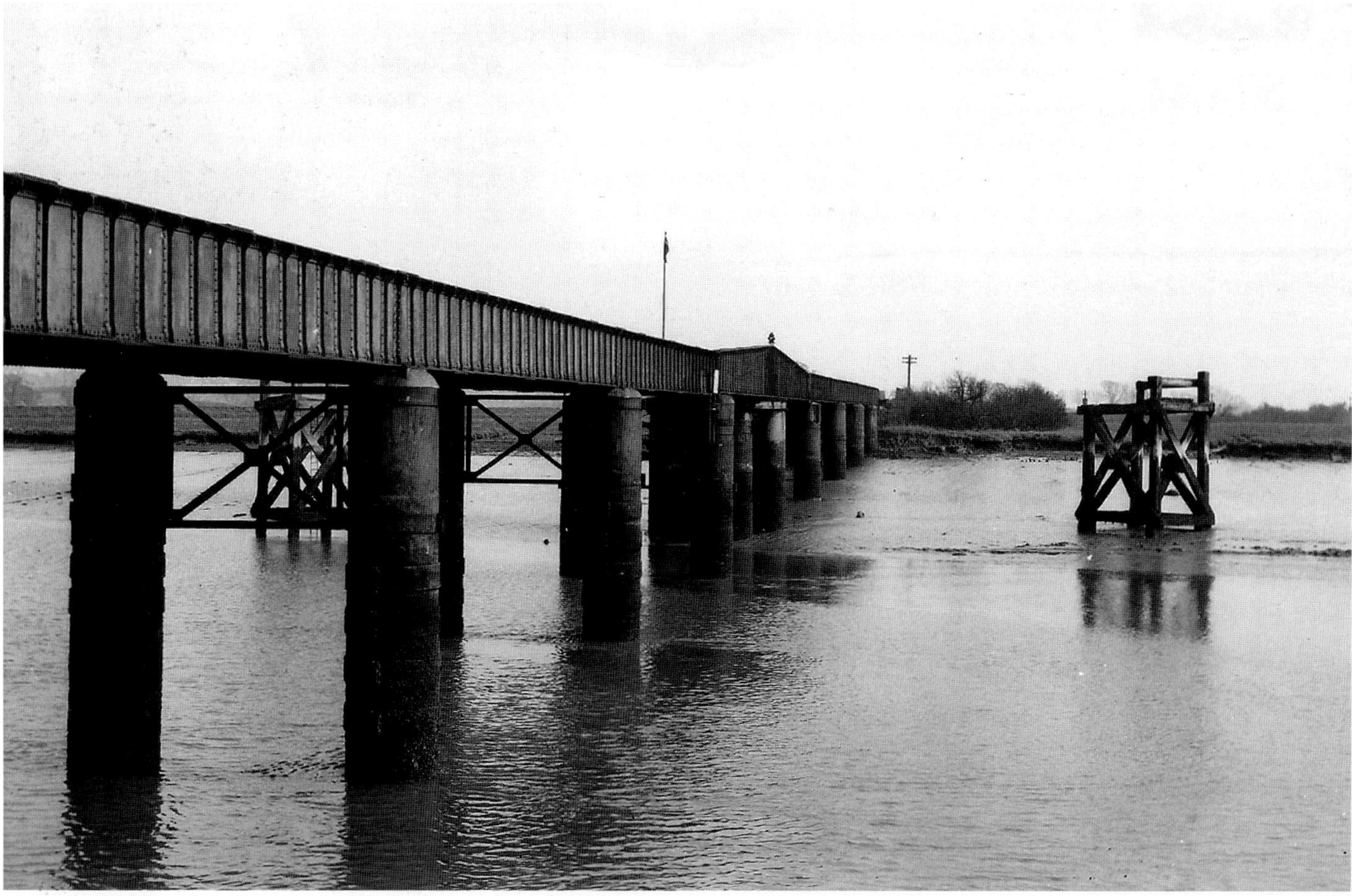

Alresford Swing Bridge over Alresford Creek (1865-1967) was 470ft long and constructed of wrought iron girder spans on cast iron cylinders. It was to a symmetrical plan, from each end one 30ft and three 50ft fixed spans, plus a 100ft centrally-pivoted swing span at the centre. This view was taken from the Wivenhoe end on 26.4.1964, shortly before the line closed. The timber piers on which the swing span rested when open can be seen. See also p.20.

John Watling